Traditional Frer
for Begi

A detailed guide to the A
including sections on surfa.
wax polishing, stripping and cleaning.

Traditional French Polishing for Beginners

L J Holmes

RSP Books

First Published 1996

© Leslie J Holmes, 1996

ISBN   0 952 7 353 0 X

published by

RSP Books
Cowsden
Worcestershire
WR7 4NX

PRINTED IN GREAT BRITAIN

The information contained in this publication is the result of much experience and is given in good faith. However, it is intended purely as a guide towards obtaining a thorough understanding of the subject. The techniques and methods contained herein should be developed using practice pieces only.

Neither the author nor publisher will accept any responsibility for any loss or damage to any piece of work as a result of information or advice contained within this publication. If a piece of work is considered to be valuable, in either a personal or a monetary sense, the advice of a professional should be sought before any restoration takes place.

CONTENTS

ACKNOWLEDGEMENTS

I would like to thank Sue Lashley for her incredible work on the word processor; Don McKay for his great skill in the darkroom; Sara Hoult for taking photographs; my proof readers for their diligence and invaluable advice; and, last but not least, my wife for her immense patience!

INTRODUCTION

As a wood finish for furniture and internal cabinet work, the traditional method of using french polish has been with us for nearly two hundred years. It stands superior to other finishes for its clarity and surface quality, and has been said to bring out the true character of the wood more than any other method. In addition to this, the whole process can be carried out by hand, without the need for any special equipment. It is this that makes it so attractive for both the small professional workshop and also the amateur woodworker and restorer.

The material itself is tough and resilient and will last an enormous amount of time given reasonable care. There are, of course, modern lacquers that are said to be more heat and liquid proof, but with these there are also disadvantages. One that is not immediately obvious is that such finishes are often difficult to repair when damaged, whereas damage on a traditionally polished surface is, in general, much easier to rectify.

To many people the term french polishing immediately conjures up a vision of a surface that is bright and shiny. This is unfortunately a misconception that has been with us since the early half of the century, when furniture with a high gloss finish was very much in fashion. In fact, the type of finish and brightness can be adjusted to suit a wide range of individual tastes and styles of furniture. The final appearance of a piece of work actually depends upon two things: the amount of polishing that is carried out and the treatment of the surface after the polishing has been finished.

Over the years a certain mystique seems to have developed around the art of french polishing, together with the inference that only a chosen few are able to possess this special talent! This isn't really so, it's just that the professional, through practice, has a better knowledge of how the material behaves when it is applied, and, due to this, a greater ability to prevent things from going wrong. The object of this book is to provide the reader with a little of this ability by offering a clear stage by stage system of work. This is in the belief that if the basics are learnt carefully there is less likelihood of problems occurring in the first place, and a much better chance of dealing with them if they do arise. Along with this, I have also endeavoured to cover the details and techniques that those new to the subject often find difficult to master.

For the greatest benefit a practice piece could be worked upon as the book is read. However, as with most technical books aimed at providing instruction, it is perhaps wise to read all the way through first, and then work on the practice piece during a second reading. A piece of either plywood or blockboard is ideal for this purpose and further details are given in the Appendix.

I have started at a point where the reader may have one of three situations to deal with: a piece of new work that has been recently made; a piece of furniture that has been stripped and is ready for polishing; or an item where the surfaces have deteriorated, not to a point where stripping is necessary, but where cleaning and re-polishing will produce a satisfactory result.

When working on existing furniture, the decision on which course to take is often not as clear cut as it might be. If the choice is a borderline one, it is usually best to try the simplest remedy first. For example, where the surfaces of a piece of furniture have deteriorated to a point where stripping might or might not be necessary, it is well worth cleaning and re-polishing a sample area as a first step. Then, depending upon the outcome of this, a further decision can be made. As a point of interest, the term re-polishing refers to re-french polishing. This is where the surface is thoroughly cleaned and re-french polished to restore its appearance. The amount of polishing necessary is obviously less than when starting with either a new or a stripped surface, and this, of course, can mean a significant saving in time and materials.

The same principle of trying the simpler method first also applies where the surface of a piece of furniture is perhaps just a little dull and worn. In this case, wax polishing a small area first will often give an indication of whether or not further action is required.

Stripping should only be carried out when the existing finish has perished to a point where it is quite clear that no other means would restore the surface. This is particularly important where a piece of antique furniture is concerned, as such an action could well spoil its appearance and reduce its value.

You will see from the contents that there are several sections allied to the main subject. The skills learnt in each one of these are of equal importance if a good quality piece of work is to be produced. Chapter 5 describes the art of french polishing itself, but it is just as important to make sure that such things as surface preparation and staining are also carried out to a high standard beforehand.

The format of the book is designed so that the basics can be learnt in a straightforward manner within Chapters 1 to 6, and then extra techniques and finer points taken on board from Chapter 7 onwards.

Although I have chosen to begin the book where the three situations previously described make a good starting point, in Chapters 7 and 8, I have included details of the stripping of old finishes and the cleaning of existing surfaces prior to re-polishing.

L J Holmes

1

BASIC PRINCIPLES

French polish is a liquid resin-type material rather like thin varnish. One of its advantages over varnish is that it dries more quickly. It is applied to the surface of the wood with a pad called a "rubber" (made from cloth and wadding). Several coats are applied. The first one or two normally soak in to the porous surface of the wood, but eventually, after perhaps four or five coats or "rubbers" as we call them, the surface starts to build up. At this point there are two things to note. Firstly, although the surface will have developed a slight sheen, the actual pores of the wood will still show up as tiny holes or depressions (often referred to as "open grain") which have not yet been filled with polish. Secondly, the path of the rubber will have left very fine streaks on the surface. The purpose of the work from this point onwards is to gradually fill the pores with polish and, at the same time, flatten out the streaks in order to produce an even, high quality finish.

The fullness of the finish, ie. the amount the pores are filled up with polish, depends largely on the amount of time and work put in. It is not however always desirable to fill the pores right up and produce a glass-like finish, such as that found on a piano. Many french polished finishes tend to be "semi-full" meaning that the pores are partially visible. A small amount of open grain showing can often produce a pleasing appearance. Some woods, oak for example, can look equally attractive with either an "open grain", "semi-open grain" or indeed "full" finish. The choice of which depends upon personal preference and also the style of the furniture.

The overall process of french polishing is not particularly lengthy, but it is made up of a number of small tasks, each requiring a specific technique but taking only a short amount of time. The trick is good planning. For example, a part that has been stained may have to be left overnight to dry before work can continue. Although the staining may only take a few minutes, it is obviously important to do this the day before you have planned to do the main volume of work.

Before going on to the actual technique of applying french polish, there are two things that must first be taken into consideration. The condition of the surface and the finished colour required. Taking these in order, we will look at surface condition in Chapter 2 and then go on to colour in Chapter 3.

2

SURFACE CONDITION

The condition of the surface prior to polishing is of prime importance, as it is impossible to produce a good quality finish on a poor surface. Whether it is a new piece of work or the re-polishing of an existing item that is to be carried out, the surface must be thoroughly examined and note taken of places that require attention, such as holes, cracks, splits, areas of coarse grain etc. Even though small defects may look fairly insignificant on bare wood, once a sheen has developed they become magnified considerably. A useful tip when carrying out such an examination, is to place a small piece of masking tape adjacent to each fault, so that none will be forgotten.

NEW WORK

Corner Splits
Corner splits of the type shown in Fig. 1 are often found on newly made pieces of work.

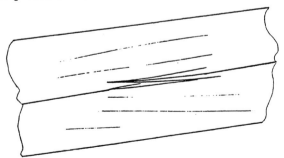

Fig. 1   *Small corner splits like this must be glued down.*

It is important that they are glued down properly and levelled with a small sanding block afterwards. The glue should be worked under the surface with a craft knife and the repair held in place with one or two thin strips of masking tape, Fig. 2. I always use Cascamite resin glue for such purposes. Wipe the surplus glue off with a damp cloth after the masking tape has been applied. Not too wet, otherwise the glue will be washed out of the repair.

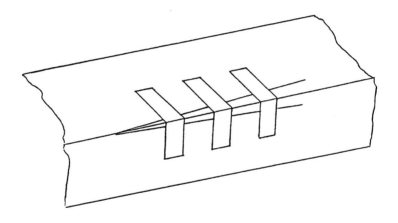

Fig. 2   *Using thin strips of masking tape to hold*
a small split in place while the glue sets.

Filling Holes and Cracks

Wood Fillers
The three main types currently popular are water based, cellulose based and resin based. The first two can be identified by their smell; water based fillers have very little smell, whereas cellulose fillers have a characteristic peardrop smell, rather like

nail varnish. Resin fillers are distinguished by the fact that they come in the form of a paste and a hardener.

Water based fillers are easy to use and are available in a good range of colours. Cellulose fillers harden more quickly but tend, in general, to be coarser and a bit fluffy. Resin fillers set quickly, though colour ranges are very limited.

There is another material that has been largely forgotten about, except by professionals, and this is "shellac stick" filler. It is available in a good range of colours and is melted into the hole using a hot iron. A small soldering iron heated over a gas ring is ideal for this purpose. The shellac stick is held just above the hole. As the tip of the hot iron is brought into contact with it, it will melt and can be dripped down onto the surface of the wood. Fig. 3.

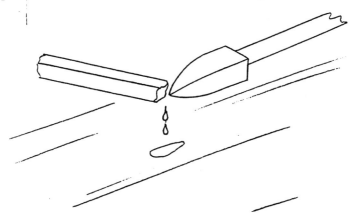

Fig. 3   The heat from a soldering iron is used to melt the
         shellac filler a small distance above the hole.

Avoid touching the surface of the wood with the iron otherwise scorching may take place. The advantage of using this material is that once it has cooled, it can be levelled down and worked upon straight away.

Do bear in mind that woodfillers and shellac stick fillers are for use on bare wood only. If used on existing polished surfaces, the sanding necessary to level them down would remove both the polish and the stain, and cause patches that are very difficult to rectify.

Stripped surfaces can be treated as bare wood but it is important to keep sanding to a minimum in order to avoid changing the colour of the surface. (Page 17)

When applying a filler, always leave a small amount of material slightly proud of the surface so that there is enough to sand level with the surrounding area. This must not, however, be an excessive amount, otherwise its removal will take longer than necessary.

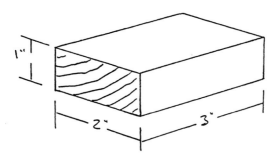

Fig. 4   *A small wooden sanding block. Make sure that all the surfaces are flat.*

For levelling woodfiller, a small wooden block approximately 3"x 2"x 1"as shown in Fig. 4 is very useful. Start by using a medium abrasive paper (180 grade) and, when the surface is nearly flat, reduce down to a finer one (320 grade) to finish off . The paper should be cut with an old pair of scissors so that it can be folded around the block as shown in Fig. 5.

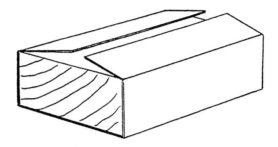

Fig. 5   *Crease the sandpaper well around the corners of the block. (further note on page 26)*

STRIPPED SURFACES

In the main, stripped surfaces can be treated in a similar way to new work. However, there is a particular point worth mentioning and this concerns colour. After a time most woods fade due to sunlight. The problem we have in this respect is that the faded top surface is only a few thousandths of an inch deep, and even the smallest amount of sanding could break through this thin layer. The result is fairly obvious, a dark area of wood from underneath will show through. Not only will this look unsightly, but if it is a piece of antique furniture that is receiving attention, a flaw such as this could spoil its appearance and very drastically reduce its value.

Woodfilling and sanding on stripped surfaces, must therefore be carried out with the greatest of care. If the holes are small they are best left alone and dealt with using wax filler at a later stage.

A further point regarding antique furniture is that holes and scratches that have developed over a long period of time often form part of the character and history of the piece concerned and, as such, should normally be left unfilled.

Bruises

Occasionally it is necessary to deal with a bruise. This is a shallow, wide indentation caused by impact from a smooth object. Damage such as this can sometimes be rectified by steaming, but this should only be carried out on either new wood or stripped surfaces and not on top of a polished finish.

A small piece of wet cloth is laid over the bruise and the area is gently heated with the tip of a hot iron, Fig. 6. The temperature of the iron should be set between medium and full. Do not let the cloth dry out, otherwise it will scorch the surface. Make sure that the iron is switched off during use as **water and electricity do not mix**. As the steam is produced the fibres of the wood will swell and, with a bit of luck, rise up. Tilt the iron so that it is only the tip that is in contact with the wet cloth. It is not advisable to attempt this on a piece of antique furniture, because, as well as raising the bruise, the steam may also bring the original darker colour up to the surface, which will once again spoil its appearance and reduce its value. Much better to leave the bruise alone and call it "character"!

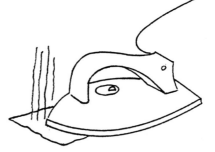

Fig. 6
Lifting a bruise with steam. Keep the iron tilted slightly so that only the tip is in contact with the surface.

CLEANED SURFACES

It is likely, after a piece of furniture has been in service for a number of years, that the finish has become dull and a little worn. Providing it is intact and there is no drastic damage, cleaning and re-polishing may be all that is necessary to restore its appearance. Stripping should only be carried out as a last resort when either wax polishing or cleaning and re-french polishing would clearly have little effect. The procedure for re-polishing is the same as that used for new wood, the difference being that less work is necessary owing to the presence of the existing finish. In order to re-polish a piece of furniture successfully, the existing surface must be perfectly clean, otherwise the new finish will not adhere properly. (See Chapter 7). After the cleaning has been done, the next step is to fill any small holes that may be present, but do remember the previous comment about the character of antique furniture.

Other forms of wear and tear such as ring marks and blemishes may also need attention before re-polishing commences; these are dealt with in Chapter 9.

The filling of holes on top of an existing finish is normally carried out using a wax filler. This is a special type of coloured wax used for small holes and cracks of up to $3/16$" (4mm) diameter. It is available in a wide range of colours to suit most woods, and different colours can also be melted and mixed together. A small aluminium foil container held over a heat source is ideal for doing this. The wax is best applied with a warm tool such as a chisel that has been carefully blunted so that it will not scratch the surface of the polish. I use an old $3/4$" (18mm) chisel kept specially for this purpose. The chisel should first be sharpened in the normal way to make sure that there are no ridges present. Then, by rubbing it on a piece of medium, and then fine, abrasive paper, take off the sharpness and also round the corners a little. A good way of warming the chisel is to hold it in hot water for a few minutes and then wipe it dry before

use.   It must not be too hot otherwise the wax will melt.   Our
intention is to soften it just enough to make it workable.   To fill a
hole, dig the corner of the chisel into the wax filler and pick up a
small amount on one corner.   Press it firmly into the hole leaving a
little above the surface, Fig. 7.

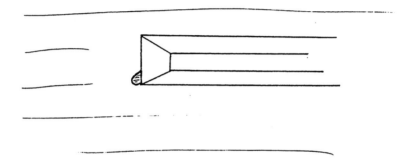

Fig. 7   *Press the wax filler firmly into the hole.*

Add more wax as necessary so that it is slightly above the
surface and then with the tool at a low angle pare away the surplus.
Fig. 8.

Fig. 8   *Pare away the surplus wax by gently pushing the
blunt chisel forwards.*

It is important that any wax that has spread around the hole, Fig. 9, is removed by lightly sanding with fine sandpaper (400 grade). The reason for this is that french polish does not adhere very well to the surface of wax, and if left this could ultimately end up as a blister or an area that would scratch easily. If a piece of partially worn paper can be found (400 grade) so much the better as this will cause less abrasion to the surface.

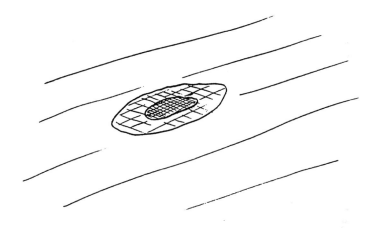

Fig. 9   *The wax smear around the hole must be removed.*
Otherwise there will be poor adhesion over this area.

The important thing to remember is to fill only the hole and to try not to spread the wax over an area any larger than necessary. The whole point of using wax filler here, as opposed to other methods of filling, is to avoid the use of coarse and medium sandpapers which would undoubtedly damage the polished surface.

Wax filler can also be used for filling small holes on surfaces that are in good condition and not actually in need of re-polishing.

In this case the wax is levelled down with the back of the sandpaper instead of the abrasive side.   Better still use a small piece of cardboard for this purpose.   This will reduce the possibility of the surface becoming damaged by small grains of abrasive that may come loose and find their way underneath the paper.

The above method is good as a simple repair, but care is needed particularly when using the chisel in order to avoid damaging the surface.

I mentioned earlier that wood fillers should only be used on bare wood.   By the same token, wax filler should only be used on polished surfaces or during the course of polishing.   The reason for this is that if used on bare wood, the wax would impregnate the surface and prevent both the absorption of stain and also the adhesion of french polish.

Always carry out the cleaning process before using wax filler, otherwise the white spirit used for cleaning will soften the wax and remove it from the holes.

SANDPAPERING

Whether the surface concerned is one that is new, one that has been stripped or otherwise one that has been cleaned ready for re-polishing, it is almost certain that sandpapering of some form will be necessary.

As pointed out by my dear friend and mentor, it is wrong to use the term sandpapering, as sandpaper went out with the Ark. However, rather like hoovering the carpet, the word seems to have firmly stuck with us. "Abrasive papering" just doesn't sound right.

The abrasive papers we use nowadays are very high-tech and are created from a variety of materials such as garnet, aluminium oxide and silicon carbide.   Such papers are available in a wide range of grades.   For general woodworking, the coarsest normally needed would be 100 grade and the finest 400 grade. Useful grades in between these are 180 and 320. There are coarser and finer grades available, but a selection such as this will normally suit most of our requirements.

When dealing with new work start with 180 grade paper and then reduce and finish with 320 grade. Surfaces that have been stripped can be lightly sanded with 320 or 400 grade, but be careful! As previously mentioned, it is so easy to break through the faded layer and cause a darker patch.

Work that has been cleaned prior to re-polishing can also be very lightly sanded using either 320 or 400 grade paper. The object here is to abrade the surface a little in order to provide better adhesion for the new polish. It is important however not to sand through the existing layer of polish. The reason for this is that, as well as the surface of the wood, the polish itself may have either faded or become a little opaque. Consequently, sanding through either whole or part of the way through the finish will almost certainly cause differences in colour.

A further reason for care in this respect is when working on fairly modern furniture. Since the 1940s most mass produced furniture has been finished using synthetic lacquers applied by spray. In many cases, instead of staining the wood first, the colour is mixed in with the lacquer. Consequently, if the lacquer is sanded too heavily in one place, the result will almost certainly be a light patch.

This would mean extra work at a later stage and such problems, including those mentioned above, are very difficult to rectify successfully.

SANDING TECHNIQUES

Use of blocks

When or when not to use a sanding block is a question that is often asked. A block should always be used for levelling woodfiller (page 16) and for the initial cleaning up of new work where the surfaces are perfectly flat. Apart from these two situations, most of the sanding we do as far as french polishing is concerned is done by hand.

On the occasions, however, when the use of a block is necessary a certain amount of caution must be applied. Cork and other soft faced sanding blocks are fine for general use, but the flexibility that they have can often be a disadvantage. Fig. 10 shows how this type of block can cause "rounding over" if too much pressure is applied when sanding over an edge. I personally prefer to change to a wooden block when sanding either over or along an edge, so that the surface is kept as flat as possible. I am sure that some might think that this is splitting hairs, but even a slight amount of roundness can be quite noticeable on a flat surface.

Fig. 10

The softness of a cork and other types of soft faced block
can cause rounding over if too much pressure is applied.

An ideal size for a general purpose wooden block would be 4"x2$^1/_2$"x1$^1/_4$". The bottom, of course, must be perfectly flat. The same applies when working on narrow surfaces, Fig. 11. The use of a small wooden block will once again prevent rounding over. It is best to use a block that is only just a little wider than the surface being sanded in order to prevent wobbling from side to side. Fig. 12.

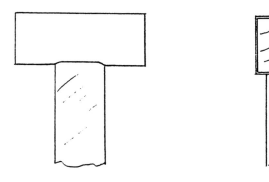

Fig. 11 *Soft blocks can also cause*   Fig. 12 *It is much better to*
roundness on a narrow edge.   *use a small wooden block.*

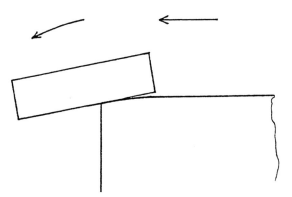

Fig. 13   *Rounding over caused by the block tipping slightly.*

Another cause of rounding over, which one must be careful to avoid, is allowing the block to tip slightly as it goes over an edge. This is very often the result of letting it travel too far over before it is pulled back, Fig. 13.

An additional point relating to blocks; after initially folding a piece of sandpaper around the block, take it off and crease the corners along the fold lines. This will produce a flatter working surface on the underside.

Hand Sanding

Hand sanding also requires a few skills that may not be immediately obvious. The paper, first of all, should be cut into quarters and then folded as shown in Fig. 14.

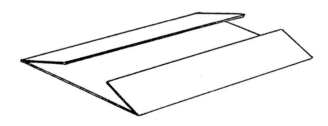

Fig. 14   *Cut the sandpaper into four and then fold in along the longest sides about $1^1/_4$" (30mm).*

Lift one corner and hold it between the thumb and first finger. The rest of the hand should be flat on top of the paper and not raised. (See photograph opposite page 48). If the fingers are raised the pressure will not be evenly distributed and the consequence of this is uneven sanding.

Round and shaped surfaces are usually dealt with by hand, but it is important, particularly where fine mouldings are concerned, not to alter the shape of the moulding by sanding too hard.

Care must be taken when dealing with corners as they must not be rounded too much, but neither must they be razor sharp. It is best during the course of "cleaning-up" to avoid sanding the corners at all and deal with them afterwards. A good way of doing this is to hold the paper between the thumb and first finger as you run along the edge. As this is done a small cavity is produced which takes the pressure off the corner itself. (See photograph opposite page 48). After the main part of the work has been completed, the corners can then have two or three light strokes with a piece of fine sandpaper which should be enough to just remove the acute sharpness and not round them too much.

This technique is also used when light sanding becomes necessary during the polishing process. In this case even greater care must be taken, as the slightest pressure on a corner can rub off, not only the polish that has been applied, but also the stain, leaving it looking light and amateurish.

When sanding along very narrow edges and into mouldings, the best method is to gently use the tips of the fingers and a small piece of sandpaper. It often helps to use the thumb as a guide in a similar manner to that described above for working near a corner.

If there is the possibility of splinters occurring and, in particular, when working on newly made items, always use short sanding strokes in order to keep injury to a minimum.

3

COLOUR

Apart from the grain and figuring naturally present in a piece of wood, it is probably the colour that first draws our attention and provides a clue towards identification. Over the years it has become popular to use a stain in order to enrich the colour and improve the finished appearance of a piece of furniture. It is not always necessary to do this and there are times when it is desirable to keep the colour of the wood as light as possible. This is of course personal choice, but in general a little staining is normally advantageous as some of the woods that we have available nowadays are much paler than their earlier counterparts. Mahogany is a good example of this, where staining is normally required in order to reproduce the rich brown/red colours of the Honduras and Cuban mahoganies of the past. Oak is also a wood that is quite often stained, either to a medium or a rich dark brown. In this case, though, it is for reasons of tradition that we have come to expect these colours, particularly when copying the designs of some of our early period furniture.

TYPES OF STAIN

There are four types of stain that we use in general: oil stains, water stains, spirit stains and chemical stains. Each of these has its own particular advantages and disadvantages.

Oil Stains

Easy to use but gloves should be worn as the solvents used could cause irritation to the skin. Must be left for at least 24 hours for the oils present to dry thoroughly before polishing. May be thinned with white spirit. Good range of colours available. Colour may fade in direct sunlight.

A point to note : beware of plastic containers and oil stain. Oil stain will dissolve certain types of plastic very quickly. The result - a well stained workbench!

Spirit Stains

Thinned with methylated spirit, not white spirit. Very useful for small areas up to 6"x 6", but very difficult, if not almost impossible, to obtain a good result on large areas. Being methylated spirit-based, the stain dries within seconds and is difficult to apply evenly. Also prone to fading.

Water Stains

Easy to apply. May be thinned with water. Good range of colours. Resists fading. Dries overnight (minimum 8 hours). However, is likely to raise the grain. (The fibres swell and rise up a little causing a slightly coarse surface). This can be prevented by "pre-raising". The surface is moistened with a damp cloth a day or so before staining. This pre-raises the grain which, after being allowed to dry thoroughly, can then be sanded down again with 320 grade paper. Pre-damping in this way usually prevents the fibres from rising again when the stain is finally applied. If there is time to do this twice, even better. Having said all this, there are water stains on the market that are specially formulated to reduce grain raising and some are very effective.

Chemical Stains

There are a number of substances that have been used for many years to change the colour of wood by chemical reaction, a popular one being bichromate of potash. It comes in the form of bright orange crystals that are dissolved in hot water. It is particularly effective on mahogany, giving it a rich red-brown colour. Results vary from wood to wood and this is an advantage to us in some cases. For example, it has very little effect on boxwood. Therefore, a piece of furniture that has been inlaid with this wood can be stained without affecting the colour of the inlay.

Another method of chemical staining is "fuming" with ammonia. Using this method, oak will turn to a very nice rich brown colour. The items to be fumed are carefully laid out in a sealed plastic bag, inside which is also placed a saucer containing a small amount of ammonia. The colour obtained will vary according to the number of days that the wood is exposed to the fumes inside the bag.

Chemicals such as these can be hazardous if used incorrectly and the beginner would be well advised to gain further information and also seek advice before using them.

STAINING TECHNIQUES

With the exception of chemical stains all of the other stains are applied using a similar technique. This is to apply the stain to the surface quickly and fairly liberally. The whole surface must be covered as soon as possible and kept moist for about 20 seconds, at the end of which time the surplus must then be rubbed off as quickly as possible, in order to produce an even colour. During this period, any areas that show signs of drying should be re-wet immediately. If any part of the surface is allowed to dry before rubbing off takes place, patches will almost certainly be produced.

It is important where flat surfaces such as table tops and panels are concerned that the whole area is done at once. To do this on a large table top two people are needed, one to apply the stain and the other to rub off the surplus. Narrow parts such as cabinet frames and chair rails are best done one at a time otherwise the stain may be left on too long before wiping off, which could cause a darker colour.

Also be careful not to overlap onto the next part otherwise double staining will occur which is unsightly. Be especially careful when using water stain on veneered surfaces, particularly old ones. If it is left on too long before wiping off it could well soak through the veneer and soften the glue. The result can be disastrous! It pays, in such cases, to keep the "wet time" down as much as possible and wipe off as soon as the surface has been evenly covered all over.

For shaped parts such as mouldings, carvings and turnings, it is usually easier to apply the stain with a brush and then rub it off in the normal way with a piece of cloth.

On flat surfaces stains are best applied using a piece of folded polisher's wadding. The cloth used for wiping off must be absorbent. Synthetics are of no use for this job. Cotton, linen, or better still cotton towelling, is ideal. When working on a large area it is best to put the stain in a small bowl so that the wadding can be dipped in quickly. Always wear gloves as some stains can affect the skin. Apart from this, multi-coloured fingers are not a pretty sight at the dinner table!

TESTING THE COLOUR

Prior to staining it is essential to make sure that the colour and strength of the stain is correct. If you want a fairly dark colour, then you could try the stain at full strength, straight out of the tin. If a medium colour is required, mix the stain one to one with the appropriate thinners, ie. water, methylated spirit or white spirit, depending on which stain is used.

Most books will tell you to test the stain in an inconspicuous place. This, of course, is fine if you are working on a chair, as you can try it on the inside of a leg. However, this is not quite so easy when re-polishing a table top for example, because all of the surfaces are in full view and the wood on the underside may well be different, which would obviously produce a different result. The only solution here is to carefully do a small test strip along one edge. **Always make the stain weaker than you think it will need to be.** You can darken it a little if necessary, but once you have applied a stain that is too dark it is extremely difficult to get it out of the wood. New work, of course, is easier to deal with, as you can keep a few offcuts of the same wood specifically for stain testing. Make sure that the test pieces have had the same amount of sanding as the original, otherwise a false impression may be created. It goes without saying that the time that the stain is kept moist on the test area must be the same as when working on the main work piece.

When working on a piece of existing furniture, it is obviously not possible to use off cuts. The best course is to test and adjust the stain on a piece of similar wood and then do a further small test on the piece of work itself as a second check. There is an important point regarding successive applications. One would assume that two applications would make the surface twice as dark. This is not always so; it all depends on the type of stain and the porosity of the wood. A second stain with an oil stain on the following day will darken the wood about the same amount again perhaps a little less. However, water and spirit stains tend to open up the pores more and a second application often results in a much darker colour. Spirit stains are the worst offenders and a second coat on some woods can be quite drastic. So, if you think another application is required, weaken the stain and, if possible, do a further test strip first.

These points refer to the strength of the stain, but it is obviously very important to also choose the correct colour. The colour ranges offered by most manufacturers tend to have fairly standard descriptions, for example, medium oak, dark oak, brown mahogany, medium mahogany, rosewood, walnut etc. Do please err on the side of caution, as one manufacturer's idea of what brown mahogany looks like is quite often different from another's. Once again, it is wise to do a test piece, and the following is a guide to doing this.

Let us look at a typical example on a piece of mahogany. The wood is Brazilian mahogany which has a fine grain but is fairly pale, and we want to produce a medium-brown mahogany colour. The colour brown mahogany is a combination of red and brown, but with more brown than red, and the chosen stain for this test is brown mahogany water stain. The finished colour does not want to be too dark, so the stain is diluted, one part water, one part stain. After applying and rubbing off, it is felt that the standard colour is just a little too red and needs to be browner. A good way of achieving this is to add to the mixture a little dark oak stain, but, before doing this, dilute the dark oak stain by the same proportion as the original stain, ie. 1 water - 1 stain. A further test should then be done and re-adjusted if necessary. This is only an example of how colours can be adjusted. Most stains can be inter-mixed, providing, of course, they are of the same type, ie. water, oil or spirit. It is not, however, possible to mix one type with another. Obviously, for test purposes only small quantities should be used.

When examining the area that is being tested, it is the colour that is seen **immediately after wiping off** that will give the nearest idea of the finished result after polishing. As the stain dries it will change colour on the surface and give a false impression which will tend to look lighter than it is in reality. If a little time has elapsed since staining and you have forgotten what the colour looks like, moisten a small area with methylated spirit. As the surface is moistened the true colour will show through for a few seconds. Do not, however, rub the surface, otherwise some of the stain will be removed. If spirit stain has been used (methylated spirit-based) it is best to do the test with white spirit as methylated spirit will remove the stain. There is a slight disadvantage here, as after using white spirit the surface must be left overnight to dry before polishing commences.

Stain testing should always be done in daylight, preferably slightly overcast or at least out of direct sunlight. Artificial light can play tricks with colours. Fluorescent lamps will make a piece of furniture look less warm or red than it really is. Ordinary tungsten light bulbs have the opposite effect and will exaggerate the amount of red present in the colour.

Staining a surface prior to applying a finish is the traditional way of deepening the colour of a piece of work. Some woods, however, do not take stain very well. Beech is a typical example, and when stained, the result is often patchy and uninteresting. This is due to the variable porosity of the surface. Many plywoods also produce a similar effect.

The only way to avoid this is to use a tinted polish instead of staining, and build up the colour during the course of the polishing process. This is accomplished by using spirit-based colours or dyes and the mixing of these is explained on pages 59-62. The strength of the tint within the polish should not be too strong otherwise streaks will be produced. The only way to achieve an even colour is to use a fairly weak mixture and a large number of thin applications. It is important, when using this procedure, that ordinary untinted polish is used for the first few rubbers (base coats), otherwise the colour will be absorbed into the wood and this will act as a stain instead of a tint, causing patchiness.

Tinting in this way can also be used to adjust the colour of a piece of work where the original staining was not quite deep enough. One of the disadvantages of using a tinted polish throughout, is that if the surface becomes scratched or badly worn, the lighter wood underneath will show through. Most modern furniture is sprayed with tinted lacquers and it is for this reason that it often looks shabby quite quickly if subjected to heavy wear and tear.

4

MATERIALS

FRENCH POLISH

French polish is a resin-type liquid, rather like thin varnish but having the added advantage of being quick drying. It is made by dissolving shellac, a material that rather resembles hard toffee, into methylated spirit. The manufacturer's art is in the blending of shellac and other additives in order to produce a polish that is the right colour, hard, and easy to use. There are four main types normally available: Button Polish, Garnet Polish, White Polish and Transparent Polish.

Button Polish

This is a general purpose product, it is orangy-brown in colour and produces a fairly hard finish.

Garnet Polish

This is a very dark polish that has been very popular in the past for piano finishing.

White Polish

A white, creamy colour, good for very light work but not very hard. Also only has a shelf life of about one year, whereas most other polishes will last for ten years or more.

Pale, Transparent Polish

A very pale golden colour. Once again useful for light work.

These are the basic types, but it is the way different

manufacturers make up these materials that gives them their individual characteristics, ie. some are better to work with than others. Before starting a piece of work, it is well to give a few minutes thought to the colour of the polish itself and how it might effect the final result. For example, on a light piece of work, button polish may produce a finish that is a little too orangy, and if this is the case a transparent polish would be a better choice. The word transparent in this context does not necessarily mean that the material is absolutely clear, but that the cloudiness has been removed which leaves the polish translucent. Colours vary from a dark honey colour to pale amber, which is almost clear in use, and good for very light work.

Ordinary button and white polishes are available from DIY hardware stores. However, you may have to shop around a little to obtain the others mentioned.

THE RUBBER

This is a small pad used to apply the polish. It is made by folding and wrapping a piece of polisher's wadding inside a piece of fine cotton cloth. Polisher's wadding looks a bit like cotton wool with a fine covering on it. Cotton wool, incidentally, should only be used as a last resort. It does not have the same characteristics as wadding and can lead to difficulties in use. The best cloth for rubber making is white cotton sheeting. Old cotton bed sheets are ideal; synthetics, such as polyester cotton, should not be used as they are too harsh.

The wadding is cut to size and folded in a particular way. After this it is placed on the cloth, which is then folded around it. The procedure is described in detail on the following pages. I have designed this method of making a rubber especially for newcomers to the subject. It takes a little longer than some other methods but is fairly simple to master.

Making the rubber
The rubber is made by first folding the wadding into shape and then covering it with cloth. It is best to do this on a flat surface such as a table. Place some newspaper down first in order to keep the materials clean. Fig. 15 below gives approximate measurements for different sizes of rubber and there is a stage by stage description and diagram on pages 38 and 39. (Also photographs opposite page 49)

Rubber Sizes			
Size	**Cloth**	**Wadding**	**Area** Up to _ sq.ft.
1	4 x 4	2 x 2	1
2	6 x 6	3 x 3	3
3	8 x 8	5 x 5	5
4	10 x 10	7 x 7	7
5	12 x 12	9 x 9	over 7

The recommendations for area are approximate and should only be used as a guide.

Fig. 15   *Sizes of materials for making rubbers (in inches).*

First cut a piece of wadding and a piece of cloth of a suitable size for the work in hand.

Fold the wadding in half towards you (1 & 2). Now fold the right hand side over a little more than 45° (3). Repeat this from the left hand side (4). The bottom corners are now folded towards the middle, but the tips are kept upright and pinched together (5, 6 & 7). Lay the cloth down and turn it diagonally. Place the wadding in the centre and pull it towards you about $3/4$"/18mm (8), and fold the cloth over along the right hand side of the wadding (9). Repeat this from the left hand side (10). There will be a surplus piece of cloth top right, fold this inside between the layers (11). Gather the cloth at the rear, and twist clockwise to finish off (12).

The above instructions are for a right handed person. For left handed people, fold the cloth at 9 from the left first, and when twisting to finish, twist anti-clockwise.

When holding the rubber, always try to keep the tips of the fingers as near the front as possible (photographs opposite page 64). The surplus cloth should be kept bunched up into the palm of the hand and not trailing on the surface of the work. Also, most beginners find that a small elastic band around the twist will help to keep the rubber in shape. (I suppose we could call this a "rubber band"!)

OIL ·

Traditionally there are two types of oil used to lubricate the rubber - raw linseed oil and white oil. My advice is to try both, as some people prefer linseed and others white. I prefer white, as I find it nicer to use and less sticky, but this is only personal choice.

These are the main materials used. Always purchase the best quality available. French polishing is an interesting skill but poor or incorrect materials can often lead to disappointment.

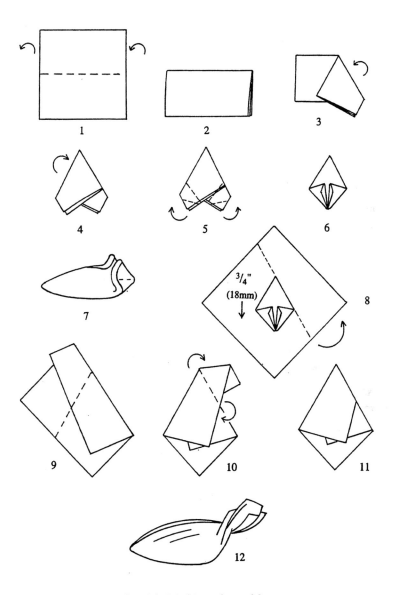

Fig. 16 *Making the rubber*

5

FRENCH POLISHING

Please bear in mind that the scheme of work here has been designed with the beginner in mind and, as such, may vary a little from other methods described elsewhere. It is a system that I have taught to many people over the years and with a little care will produce very good results.

As outlined earlier, the basic object is to fill, or partly fill, the pores of the wood and flatten the surface of the polish in order to produce a smooth even finish. Initially, four or five rubbers or coats of french polish are applied at, say, fifteen minute intervals. The first one or two rubbers will appear to have soaked right into the surface, but after four or five coats a sheen will start to develop. If you run your hand over the surface about fifteen minutes after the last coat, it will feel quite dry, but it is not actually very hard, and we use this "cheesy" stage to our advantage. Whilst the polish is in this sort of semi-hard state we are able to push it into the pores and press it flat, and this is the principle behind french polishing.

In broad terms the rubber is moistened with french polish and rubbed around in circles on the surface. This may sound simple enough in principle, but if attempted at this point it would just stick, causing a dreadful streaky mess. In order to be able to work the rubber without this happening, a means of lubrication is necessary and is achieved by applying a little oil to the face of the rubber. This forms a microscopic film on the surface which allows us to work the rubber freely without the risk of sticking. These are the basics.

Before going into the finer details of each stage, let us now take a look at the whole procedure from start to finish. Initially, a few (4 - 6) thin layers of french polish are applied to form a base to work on. A few more rubbers of polish are then applied, but now, after each time the rubber is charged with polish, a little oil is added. This gradually forms a film over the surface. Once the film is present all over, it is then safe to work the rubber around in circles. This is done between 5 and 10 times over the whole surface. Working in circles like this is what we call "bodying-up", which is the main part of the process. Following this, the oil must be removed. Its use is discontinued and the rubber is then returned to straight runs with polish only. By doing this, the remaining oil on the surface is absorbed into the rubber. Finally, to make absolutely sure that all the oil has been completely removed, a fresh, clear rubber (clear of oil) is run once or twice over the surface and the job is finished. I shall go over this again in more detail, but first there are a few points that must be considered.

The amount of fullness produced depends on the number of circles worked with the rubber, but it is wise not to work too many at once otherwise the polish will be built up too quickly without giving the preceding layers enough time to harden. For the beginner, five sets of circles at a time is ideal, after which the work can be put aside for a few hours to harden. I call this "resting" the work.

The oil does not always have to be removed straight away after bodying-up. For example, if you are going to rest the work for just an hour or so, it can be left on; however, it must not be left on overnight, otherwise there is a possibility of dull streaks appearing that are difficult to remove.

After resting for a few hours the surface will have hardened-up sufficiently for work to continue if time is critical. It is much better however, if time permits, to leave it overnight or even for a couple of days, as ultimately, a much better quality finish will be produced. The reason is as follows: even though the polish appears initially to dry quite quickly, it actually goes on drying and hardening for a considerable time afterwards. As the polish is applied most of the methylated spirit in it evaporates, which leaves the surface feeling dry, but a small amount is still present which takes longer to work up through the surface. As it evaporates out of the polish, the surface shrinks by the same amount. This is why, when you pick up a piece of work the following day after the first bodying-up, it will appear less full than it did when it was left the day before. This, we call "sinking". Obviously, if it is a semi-open grain finish that you want to produce, this may not matter too much, but, if you are working towards a fairly full finish, further bodying-up will be necessary. If between each stage of bodying-up the resting periods were quite short, a much greater sinking will occur after the work has been finished, but this may not be apparent until several days afterwards.

CHARGING THE RUBBER

The polish is put in a clean, dry jar and thinned with a little methylated spirit. A good start for thinning is four parts of polish to one part methylated spirit. Bear in mind that the thickness of different makes and types of polish will vary a little and so this is only a general guide. After some experience has been gained the polish can be made a little thinner but it is unwise to go below three to one. Probably the best way to judge the thickness is by eye. Lift the brush above the jar and allow the polish to run back down. It should be approximately the same thickness as ordinary milk. A little thicker is acceptable but certainly not any thinner at this stage.

A brush is needed, not for coating the polish but as a means of applying it to the rubber, and this we call the dipping brush. Whilst a clean paint brush will do as a temporary measure, it should really be a soft hair brush. This is much nicer to use as it will hold a good quantity of material. Soft hair polisher's brushes or "mops", as they are called vary in quality, the better ones being quite expensive.

Occasionally there is a need to apply french polish with a brush on awkward areas and for this purpose only a good quality fine hair polisher's mop should be used, the lower grades being more suitable as dipping brushes. Polisher's mops are available in a range of sizes from 4 - 18. A size 12 makes a good general purpose dipping brush, but a larger one would be useful if much work using large rubbers is contemplated. (Photograph opposite page 48)

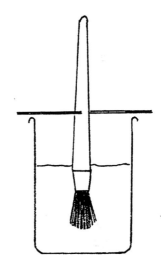

Fig. 17
A piece of stiff wire through the handle will keep the brush clear of the bottom of the jar.

Ideally the dipping brush should have a hole drilled through it to take a piece of stiff wire, which is positioned so that the hairs are a short distance above the bottom of the jar, Fig. 17. This keeps the hairs straight and also prevents the brush from picking up sediment and grime that inevitably collects from time to time. When polish brushes have been finished with for the day, they should be cleaned in methylated spirit, the hairs stroked into their natural shape and then stored upside down in an empty jar. Before doing this, the surplus polish should be removed. This is done by pulling the brush upward and gently pressing the hairs between your first finger and the edge of the jar.

It is wise to have some newspaper down on the work table in case of spills. Hold the rubber over the jar, lift the brush up and coat the bottom of the rubber three times fairly liberally, allowing any drips to run back into the jar. Have a piece of old sandpaper ready, turned upside down (abrasive side down), and with the hand flat on top of the rubber squash the polish out onto the paper. (Photographs opposite page 64). If you haven't now raced off to buy a pair of rubber gloves, mop the polish up again into the rubber. Repeat this 3 - 4 times, squashing out and mopping up. We call this, believe it or not, "squashing out", and the purpose here is to make sure that the polish is evenly distributed throughout the rubber. A new rubber being charged for the first time will require quite a lot of polish, maybe 6 - 8 coats with the brush for a size 3 rubber, using a size 12 dipping brush. Knowing exactly how much polish to charge the rubber with will come with a little practice. It must not be too wet, just moist. After charging, tap it on the back of your hand; you should only feel a little moisture. If the polish oozes out, it is much too wet and the best thing to do is to squeeze it out over the jar. It is important to make sure that every bit of polish is mopped up, otherwise small lumps of half dry polish will be picked up by the rubber and deposited on the surface. Always check the face of the rubber before applying it to the work.

How wet should the rubber be? It should contain enough polish to cover a reasonable area before re-charging is necessary, but on no account should it be too wet. Do remember that the object is to apply a very thin, even layer and not a stream that resembles a tributary of the Amazon. Some people, it seems, are convinced that applying a lot of polish speeds up the job. This is not so, in fact, the reverse happens. Applying too much at once causes the surface to be uneven and then a great deal of time and effort is needed to flatten out the ridges and ripples caused by excessive application.

Gloves can be used and the best ones are the thin, disposable, vinyl type. It is wise to discard them after a day's use. The reason for this is that the polish becomes hard after a while and if used a second time will flake off onto the surface of your work.

We will now look at the actual technique of polishing stage by stage as if this were a first practice session, using a practice board similar to that shown in the Appendix.

BASE RUBBERS

The first step is to apply 4 or 5 rubbers of polish to the surface - as a base to work on. These are put on at approximately 15 minute intervals.

We will assume for this exercise that it is a flat surface that is being polished. The rubber must land gently on the surface a little way in from the edge, travel along and then off again at the far end. I call this the "aircraft carrier" technique. Another strip follows, slightly overlapping the first one, and so on, until the surface has been completely covered. Imagine the rubber is an aeroplane, it flies in slowly, goes along the surface, takes off again, turns and then comes in from the other direction to repeat the operation. Fig. 18.

Note that when landing, rather like the aeroplane, the rubber must land a little way in from the edge, Fig. 19, otherwise a run will be produced down from the corner. **Make sure that the rubber is moving when it lands.** What you must not do is place the rubber on the surface first and then start to move it. The rubber must never be stationary, not even for a split second. Don't worry about the bits you keep missing. For some reason they always seem to get covered up eventually!

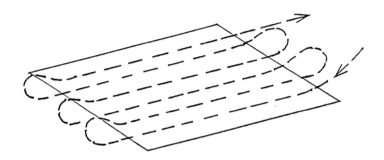

Fig. 18   *Each path of the rubber should slightly overlap the previous one.*

Fig. 19   *The rubber should land slightly in from the edge, a, travel along the surface and go straight off at b.*

After one pass across the surface, leave the work to dry for about 15 minutes and then repeat the operation. After the second rubber, leave the work for a further 15 minutes and lightly ease down with very fine (400) sandpaper. Dust the surface and then follow with a further two rubbers, also at 15 minute intervals. It does not matter at all if the intervals between the rubbers are longer. In fact, the longer the better at this stage. It is not necessary to re-charge the rubber at the beginning of each sequence. Keep using it until it starts to feel dry and only then re-charge it. Apply three coats of polish to the face of the rubber, squash out well and then continue where you left off.

In between coats, the rubber should be kept in a clean, dry jar to prevent it from drying out. If stored like this after finishing the work, rubbers can be kept for a week or more. A teaspoon of meths in the jar helps to keep them moist but must not be added whilst work is in progress, otherwise it will over-dilute the polish.

I am often asked "How long should a rubber last?" Well, it should certainly last for a few days' worth of work, even if the outer cloth has to be changed once or twice. If only used for a short period, it can be kept for further use as detailed above. The important thing is that it should always have a little bit of "spring" to it. After a time the wadding will become compressed and lose its springiness. When this happens it will hold very little polish and it will also be more difficult to control the amount of polish leaving the rubber. Once this point has been reached it is best to discard it and make up a fresh one.

BODYING-UP

Considered as the most difficult part of the job, bodying-up is where the polish is manipulated by working around in circles in order to fill the pores and produce a quality finish. Like many skills, it probably appears more difficult than it really is. The important thing is to know what is happening as you work through the various stages.

As explained earlier in the chapter, a small amount of oil is used to prevent the rubber from sticking to the surface. The oil is only used for lubrication purposes and does not form part of the finish; therefore, when bodying-up has been completed, it must be removed. An excess of oil can sometimes be difficult to remove, so it is important to use just enough and no more. Having said this, too little can also lead to problems. The following procedure will hopefully provide a good starting point and a 'feel' for the amount of oil necessary.

Applying the oil
Returning to the point where we left off; after the base rubbers have been applied we can now start to use a little oil. Continue applying straight rubbers as before, but each time the rubber is charged with polish, a small amount of oil is added **afterwards**. 4 - 6 sequences or passes over the surface will be necessary to make sure that the oil is spread evenly. The time between these rubbers can be reduced to ten minutes. On no account should oil be put on the rubber before polish as this will not work. If after a few passes the rubber starts to feel a bit dry, it should be re-charged with polish, squashed out and a further small amount of oil applied. The amount required will vary according to the size of the rubber and the surface area of the work. A little oil should be put into a small container such as a jam jar lid. It is applied by dipping a finger into this and then smearing it onto the face of the rubber. As a starting point this should be done twice after each 'charging' and 'squashing out'. This is about the right quantity for an average size of rubber, perhaps size 3, (page 37). An alternative method of applying the oil is to put it in a small bottle. After the rubber has been charged and squashed out, place the face

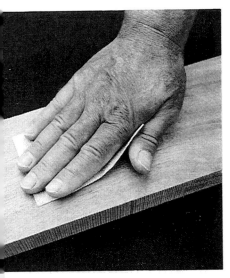

Hand sanding. The whole hand must be flat on the surface.

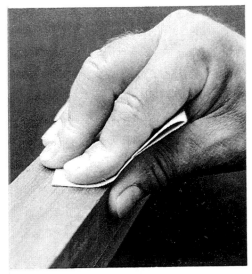

By creating a cavity with the thumb and first finger, the corner is protected.

Brushes, left to right. Small pencil brush, colouring brush, polisher's mop and dipping brush.

A selection of rubbers of different sizes.

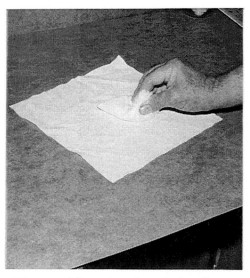

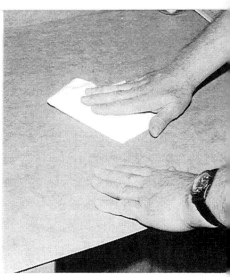

The wadding is placed in the middle of the cloth and pulled back about $3/4''$.

During the course of folding, press down flat to keep everything in shape.

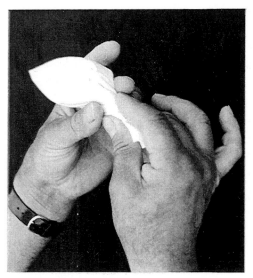

Twist the surplus cloth at the rear, being careful not to squash the rubber out of shape.

The surplus cloth should then be tucked up into the palm of the hand.

of the rubber on top of the bottle and then turn both items upside down and back again and this will leave a measured amount of oil on the rubber. I usually follow this by rubbing gently on the back of the hand to spread the oil more evenly on the face of the rubber. The back of a second piece of sandpaper could be used instead but on no account should oil be allowed to get on to the sandpaper you use for squashing out.

During the course of bodying-up the rubber will require less polish than it did during the preliminary stages. We started with three brushes for the base coats and this can now be reduced to two. So this simplifies things a little. Two coats of polish, squash out and mop up four times, then two dabs of oil. The quantity of polish and oil may need to be reduced further still if the surface area is small, ie. less than two square feet. In this case a reduction down to one brush of polish and one dab of oil would be about the right amount. This would also suit our workpiece.

After one or two passes over the surface a sort of misty trail will be seen to follow the rubber. This is called the "jet stream" and once present all over, shows us that the oil has been evenly applied. In order to help to spread the oil evenly, start from the opposite side at the beginning of each sequence. I call this "alternating". Where a large area of work is concerned, it is quite a good idea to start from the centre once or twice and work outwards. This will further help to spread an even film. Don't forget, up to this point straight rubbers, "aircraft carrier" style. If the jet stream is slow to appear, the amount of oil used may need to be increased a little.

When carrying out the initial passes using oil, keep the interval between each one to a minimum of ten minutes. After four sequences have been applied, leave the work for a further ten minutes to harden up a little before continuing

Once the oil has been applied and there is an even film on the surface there is no longer a risk of sticking, providing the rubber is kept moving. It is now that bodying-up proper can begin.

Land the rubber on the surface and start working in circles of about 2" diameter. (This being for a size 3 rubber and on an area of 2 - 3 sq.ft.). Each circle should half overlap the previous circle and each line of circles should slightly overlap the previous one. Fig. 20.

A gentle pressure is required to start with, and this is increased gradually as the rubber is used to maintain an even flow of polish.

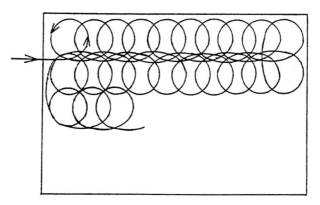

Fig. 20   *Each circle should half overlap the previous one and each line of circles should overlap the previous line.*

Continue working over the surface for several passes at five minute intervals until the rubber starts to feel dry - this is called **working the rubber out**. Then re-charge with polish and oil and continue further. If you are working on a large area that takes more than five minutes to cover, then bodying-up can be almost continuous. It is a good idea occasionally to make the first line of circles smaller than the rest. This will effectively move the whole pattern across a little and further help towards an even distribution of work.

In between each sequence put the rubber back in its jar for a few minutes. This will keep it soft. If it is left out, it will start to harden.

An extra tip where re-charging is concerned: instead of continuing straight away from the point where you left off, it is a good idea to make a couple of light sweeps across the whole surface first. This is yet another way of helping to spread the film of oil evenly. It is not necessary to do this every time, perhaps every third time you re-charge. Also, it is a particularly useful technique if you think that perhaps you might have put too much oil on the rubber, as this will disperse it across the surface as opposed to leaving it all on one place.

You may wonder, when we have already put a layer of oil on the surface, why we still need to add it to the rubber. The reason is that as the rubber is worked upon the surface it absorbs a small amount of oil all the time, and this must be replaced in order to maintain the film. If insufficient is added, and the film breaks down, the rubber will start to pull and could easily tear the soft polish and produce a dull streak.

Regardless of how many times you have to re-charge the rubber (it may only be once or twice), stop after you have passed over the whole surface five times. For a first practice piece this amount of bodying-up will be sufficient and concludes this stage of the process.

Please do not be put off if your practice piece on plywood or blockboard does not look quite as full as you might expect. Some of these materials are extremely porous and you will be pleasantly surprised how much quicker the finish builds up on solid wood. Of course, after this initial practice run, you can always body-up again once or twice for a fuller finish.

Removing the oil
After the bodying-up has been done the remaining task is to

remove the oil from the surface and **from this point on the use of oil is discontinued**. Removing the oil is accomplished by rubbering straight up and down a few times and then changing the rubber for a "clear" one and then repeating this again. A clear rubber is one that has not had any oil on it, only polish, and is thus "clear" of oil.

The procedure is as follows: with the same rubber used for bodying-up, continue working straight up and down (aircraft carrier style) 2 - 3 times with a fairly firm pressure. The polish at this point can now be made thinner - 2 parts polish, 1 part meths. When the rubber dries out re-charge with a little **polish only** (one brush) and continue. The effect of this is that the oil on the surface will gradually be absorbed by the rubber, and you will notice that the jet stream that follows the rubber when there is oil present will eventually disappear. You will also feel the rubber pulling a little (I hope) and this is another clue that the oil is being removed. If the rubber starts to feel dry, re-charge it with just a little polish only (one brush) and continue. Do bear in mind, as there is less oil on the surface and reduced lubrication, the time between each rubber must now be increased gradually back up to 15 minutes. The rubber that has been used up to this point will now have become quite contaminated with oil, and is unlikely to remove every trace from the surface. To achieve this a fresh "clear" rubber is charged with a little thin polish (2 parts polish to 1 of methylated spirit) and passed over the surface once or twice at 15 minute intervals to finish off. The ideal rubber for this purpose is not a brand new one, but one that has been used a few times with polish only (perhaps for some base coats) so that the shape has formed and the face has become soft.

The above system will usually remove the oil quite satisfactorily, and the work is then complete. If, however, there is still an indication of oil being present, ie. some jet streams (perish the thought), it probably means that there was too much used during the bodying-up stage. In this case repeat the last procedure again with another fresh clear rubber and this will almost certainly do the trick. It is wise, however, to leave the surface for about 30 minutes before doing this, so that it will have chance to harden up a little.

It is often difficult to tell whether or not the oil has been completely removed; however, there is an old method of testing for its presence. This is to breathe heavily down onto the surface. Then look quickly across and you will see the bloom caused by your breath. If it is uniform, the chances are the oil has been removed successfully. Otherwise, you will see traces of oil appearing as streaks through the bloom.

Our aim when removing the oil is to pass the rubber over the surface as little as possible. The more this has to be done, the more fine rubber streaks are produced, which will eventually spoil the flat, streak-free surface that bodying-up will have achieved.

As mentioned earlier, it is important to use only just enough oil to keep the rubber lubricated. Too little and you could either tear the surface or produce circular rubber marks. Too much and it becomes difficult to remove. It is a fine balance that will come with a little practice.

The above method of removing the oil is called "stiffing-up". I believe the reason for this is that as the oil is reduced the rubber starts to pull and is said to become stiffer.

Leave the work to harden overnight (resting the work, page 41) and examine it the following day. If it is "full" enough for your purposes, put it aside to harden for a few days before wax polishing. If a fuller finish is required, ease down with 400 grade paper (worn, if possible) and repeat the above process.

The work described so far covers the basic system of french polishing and Fig. 21 shows this stage by stage. We can now expand upon this and I shall go on to deal with some further relevant points and techniques.

Stage	No. of Rubbers	Dilution of Polish
Base rubbers	4 straight clear	4 : 1
Applying oil	4 straight with oil	4 : 1
Bodying-up	5 circles with oil	4 : 1
Removing oil	3 straight no oil	2 : 1
Finishing	2 straight clear (Fresh rubber)	2 : 1

Fig. 21   *The Basic System*

The first one is the use of figures of eight as well as circles and this is something that the beginner can practise as time goes on but is not essential initially.

Fig. 23 shows the same stage by stage system shown in Fig. 21, but with the addition of two sets of figures of eight before and after bodying-up.   Prior to bodying-up it has two effects: it further helps

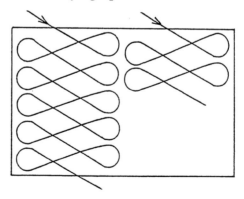

Fig. 22   *A set or two of figures of eight is advantageous before and after bodying-up.*

Stage	No. of Rubbers	Dilution of Polish
Base rubbers	4 straight clear	4 : 1
Applying oil	4 straight with oil	4 : 1
Figures of eight	2 sets with oil	4 : 1
Bodying-up	5 circles with oil	4 : 1
Figures of eight	2 sets with oil	4 : 1
Removing oil	3 straight no oil	2 : 1
Finishing	2 straight clear (Fresh rubber)	2 : 1

Fig. 23   *The same system but with the addition of a couple of sets of figures of eight before and after bodying-up.*

to spread the oil more evenly and also smoothes out the transition between straight runs and circles. After bodying-up another one or two sets would be applied and this assists the transition from circles back to straight runs.

Speed is a thing that must be given some thought. Not too fast and not too slow. I have seen people rubbing furiously in an attempt to produce a quicker finish. This does not work. In fact, there is a very good chance of tearing the surface. The correct speed should be nice and steady, with a fairly firm pressure on the rubber. Although this is perhaps rather difficult to explain, a rough guide when going straight would be about 1 foot per second, and when bodying-up 1 circle per second. So, if you were counting steadily you would do either five straight feet or five circles for the count of five.

As bodying-up progresses it is important to monitor the amount of oil present and keep it down to a workable minimum. One way of doing this is to pass a finger tip over a part of the surface. If the amount of oil picked up is significant, the chances are it needs reducing. Remember, though, that oil must always be applied after each re-charging even if it is only a small amount.

The choice of work place is important - it should be dry and reasonably warm, 60°-65° Fahrenheit, 15°-20° Centigrade. Normal room temperature is fine. Moisture in the form of humidity is our arch enemy and will cause the polish to "chill" (milky streaks). A garden shed on a dry day is the summer ideal, but the same shed on a wet day in November would be totally unsuitable, and in such conditions work should be transferred indoors. Keep the work away from anything that generates moisture such as cooking, washing machines, damp towels etc.

There is a technique often used by professionals called "fadding", which is a means of applying the base coats quickly. Instead of using a rubber, a fad is used. This is a piece of old wadding that has been previously used in a rubber. It is left to dry out completely and go hard, after which it is re-softened with polish and then kept for use in an airtight container. The fad is used on its own without any cloth around it and, consequently, the polish can be pushed out at a fairly fast rate. In skilled hands, a fad can be very useful, but if you are not careful it is very easy to produce wisps, which are heavy streams of polish rather like horizontal runs, and these are extremely difficult to remove. Although not all that apparent at the time, they often show up more as the work is nearing

completion. So during these early stages it is far better for the
beginner to use a rubber throughout.

For simplicity I have described this system of polishing as it
would be used on a wide surface such as a table top. Of course, on a
piece of furniture there are many narrow parts where it would be
impossible to work in circles even with the smallest of rubbers.
These parts are bodied-up using what I call the "shuffle". Quite
simply once the oil has been applied, instead of circles the rubber is
shuffled backwards and forwards working its way slowly along from
one end to the other, so that each area is rubbed about four times on
each pass of the rubber. Fig. 24.

Fig. 24   *On narrow edges, instead of circles, the rubber is
shuffled backwards and forwards as it works its way along.*

In general, when using the rubber, beware of runs behind
corners that you cannot see. It always pays, after completing a
section of work, to lightly run one's fingers around the edges, just to
make sure that there aren't any runs present. (Further details in
Chapter 9).

No matter how clean you are, it occasionally happens that a speck of dust finds its way on to the surface unnoticed, and this forms a pimple on the polish. The only thing to do is to put the work aside for an hour or so and then carefully level it down with some worn 400 grade paper. Smear the face of the sandpaper with white oil as this will act as a lubricant and help to reduce scratching. After the speck has been removed, wipe the area with a soft cloth to remove the excess oil.

It is very seldom that we use a brush to apply french polish, but having said this, there are occasions when awkward areas and mouldings cannot be successfully polished with a rubber. For such purposes a small soft hair polishing mop is used (see photograph opposite page 48). Ordinary paint brushes are of no use as they are much too coarse and will not hold or apply the polish correctly.

In addition to the basic system described so far, there are two further operations that are carried out during the course of the polishing process. These are the filling of small holes and the touching-up and colouring of areas that do not match the rest of the surface. Both of these procedures are carried out during the initial stages of work before bodying-up takes place. (See Systems of Work pages 135-136)

FILLING SMALL HOLES

In Chapter 2 we looked at the filling of holes using woodfiller, either on new wood or on surfaces that have been stripped. On such surfaces before a finish has been applied, small holes are often difficult to detect, but during the course of polishing they will show up and must be filled. Ordinary woodfiller is unsuitable, as it would have to be sanded with coarse paper which would cause a perforation through both the polish and the stain. We therefore use wax filler for this purpose. It is used in exactly the same way as it would be used on existing furniture being prepared for re-polishing. (Chapter 2, pages 19-22). The important thing to remember here, though, is that the surface must be hard enough to work on, otherwise the first few layers of polish will become damaged, leaving further problems to deal with. Owing to this, it is wise to leave the surface for at least two hours to harden before wax filling takes place. If, however, grainfilling has been carried out and only one or two rubbers applied since, the time can be reduced to one hour. The reason for this is that the surface will already have been left overnight for the grainfiller to harden. (Details on grainfilling in Chapter 9).

The same rules apply as when working on an existing polished surface. Do not let the wax spread too far and make sure that any surplus that has spread around the hole is removed. (Chapter 2. page 21).

Following wax filling, the surface should receive two rubbers of polish in preparation for touching-up and colouring.

TOUCHING-UP and COLOURING

These are similar operations, the difference being the size of the area in question. The object is to tone down areas that are lighter than they should be. Touching-up, or re-touching as it is sometimes called, refers to working on small marks, for instance where filler has been used and the colour of the filler is not quite dark enough. This is done with a small artists-type brush. "Colouring" or "colour-matching", to give it its correct title, indicates a larger area. For example, on a table top that is made up of several boards, one of these may be lighter than the others even after staining darker in the first place, Fig. 29, page 65. This would then need to be corrected so that it will match the rest of the table. In such a case a thin tinted polish is made up. We usually refer to this as "colour" and this is applied either with a rubber or alternatively a soft hair brush. Whichever is used to apply the material, the colour itself must not be too strong. A better job will be achieved by putting on several weak coats as opposed to one strong one.

The materials used are translucent spirit dyes that are mixed together to produce the required colour. The most useful to us are red and black. Mixed in different proportions a large range of wood colours can be made. Others available are yellow, blue and green. Green is also very useful, as a small amount is required when mixing a colour to match walnut. In addition, a mixture of weak green on its own can be used to correct an area that may have too much of a reddish tone to its appearance.

The reason they are called spirit dyes is because they are methylated spirit-based, which means that they can be used in conjunction with french polish. Even though we refer to them as red, black, green, yellow etc. they can vary a little from supplier to supplier. These products are available in either liquid or powder form. If using powder, it must be dissolved in methylated spirit to make a concentrated solution and then diluted further as required. A small amount of french polish (approximately 10%) should be added to the concentrate to act as a binder. As well as the spirit colours, one or two brushes are required. A good quality soft hair mop, about size 8, is ideal for colouring small areas. For touching-up a size 3 and a size 5 artists-type pencil brush will cover most situations.

Lets go through the sequence of mixing a colour using red and black to match, say, a medium oak. The items required are a piece of scrap wood with a 6" strip of masking tape stretched along it, a small brush, some newspaper, spirit red and spirit black concentrate and five plastic cups. (Yoghurt pots are ideal but they must be clean and dry). (Photograph opposite page 65)

First place the newspaper down to protect the work table. Pour a small amount (a teaspoonful or less) of red and black into each of the first two cups. In the third cup put a small amount of half polish and half methylated spirit. In the fourth cup a little methylated spirit for brush cleaning. The fifth cup is for mixing in.

Dip your pencil brush (a small, fine brush) into the black and drip a spot of this into the mixing cup. Rinse the brush quickly in methylated spirit, wipe on a piece of cloth and then repeat with a little red. Mix both colours together and brush a small amount on to the masking tape. Now, this is almost certain to be too strong, so before going any further add a brushful or two of the polish-meths mixture to weaken it. Do another test. Look at the colour very carefully and decide whether it is too red or too black. Whichever it is, add a little of the opposite colour and do another test. Re-adjust if necessary. This may sound long-winded but can be done quite quickly with a little practice.

Although I have chosen medium oak as the above example, the type of wood is really immaterial as the same procedure applies whatever the colour required. It is the proportions that are different. Mahogany, for instance, would need more red than black. A dark Tudor oak would require more black than red and so on. For some woods the addition of other colours is also necessary. A modern teak colour would need the red and black to be very weak, plus a very small amount of yellow. A similar mix would be necessary for satinwood, and walnut, as mentioned previously, usually requires the addition of a little green.

Before starting the mix, look at the colour that is to be copied very carefully. Is it a colour that can be made by combining red and black or is there a hint of green or a hint of yellow present? Once this initial decision has been made, the appropriate materials can be combined as described above.

It is difficult to give a precise guideline on the strength of the colour to use, but as a rough guide for touching-up, gauge the mixture so that you will achieve the correct level of colour in say 3-4 applications. For colour-matching of large areas, it should be much weaker and a greater number of coats applied, perhaps 4-6, in order to produce an even surface that is free from streaks. There are one or two little tricks that can help immensely, particularly where touching-up is concerned. First of all there are two ways of touching up a small light patch. One is by using long strokes with the brush, Fig. 25, and the other is by covering the area with small dots of colour. The use of strokes is more suitable for larger areas, whereas building up the colour with a series of dots is a useful technique for work on small marks and scratches. Fig. 26.

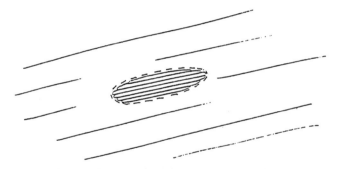

Fig. 25   *Touching-up made up of long strokes.*

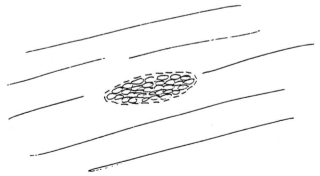

Fig. 26   *Touching-up using small dots.*

Whichever method is chosen, it is important not to have the brush too wet, otherwise a dark edging will form around each area of colouring rather like small moon craters. Fig. 27.

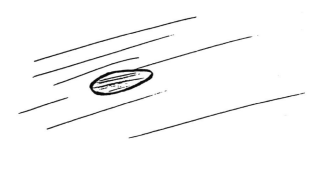

Fig. 27   *If the colour is put on too wet, a dark ring will form around the edge of each application.*

If you feel you have applied a little too much in one spot, tap the area very quickly with the tip of your finger and the chances are, rather like blotting paper, you will have taken approximately half of the colour off. The proof will be on the end of your finger! (Photograph opposite page 65). After each coat of colour has been applied, leave it to dry for at least 15 minutes before applying another, otherwise there is a risk of softening the previous ones and causing an undesirable mess. It is very important to make sure that your colouring stays within the area necessary. If it overlaps even a small amount onto the surrounding surface, a dark area will be produced. Fig. 28.

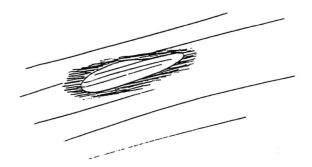

Fig. 28   *A dark area will be produced if the touching-up*
is allowed to overlap the surrounding surface.

Colour-matching, as opposed to touching-up, varies a little in technique owing to the fact that the areas being dealt with are larger.

Let us take two common situations and go through the procedure of correcting each one. The first one is a table top made up of several boards, one of which is lighter than the others, Fig. 29, and the second is a piece of veneer that has been replaced on the front of a drawer, Fig. 30. These are, of course, only examples. The same procedures apply equally to any situation where one area is lighter than another.

The table top first. It should be standing on the floor in its normal position and, if possible, in daylight as opposed to artificial light. (Pages 34 & 66)

The surface area of the board that needs correcting will be too large to use a brush, so a rubber must be used to apply the colour. Make up sufficient colour in a jar as described on page 61. Don't worry about the strength of the mixture initially, but concentrate on producing a good colour match. Once this is achieved, it can then be weakened with 50/50 polish and methylated spirit ready for use with the rubber.   It is a little difficult to describe how strong the mixture

When charging the rubber, it should be held over the jar.

Squashing out. It is important to mop up all the polish.

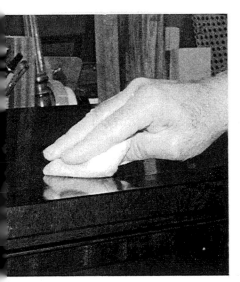

Holding the rubber. The fingers should be as near the front as possible.

Inside a moulding. The tip of the rubber must be pressed up to the moulding. Keep moving when doing the corners.

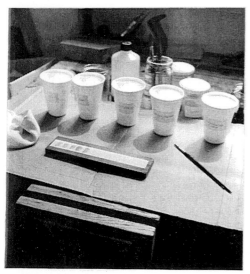

Materials for colouring. The pots are red, black, green, polish/ meths and one for mixing.

Touching-up a piece of stringing. The brush must not be too wet.

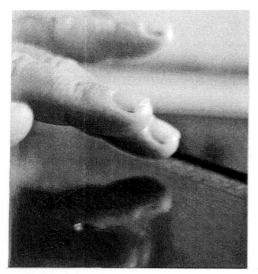

If the result is too dark, tap the area with the tip of your finger.

Colouring a small light area using a size six brush.

should be. However, if you were to make a strong cup of black coffee, let it cool a little, put it in a glass and hold it up to the light, this would give a fairly good indication of the strength required. You can always make it a bit stronger as you go on, but if you apply a colour that is too strong to start with, the result will be unsightly streaks that are virtually impossible to remove.

Using a brush, charge the rubber and squash out, and apply a rubber or two to the surface. The most important thing when doing this is to make sure that the first and last passes along the edge of the darker boards are controlled accurately. If the colour is allowed to overlap onto the darker surface, eventually a dark line will be produced along the joint.

After a couple of rubbers have been applied, leave the work for 10 minutes and do something else for a while. On returning, take note of your first impression. Is the colour about right or is it either a little too red or a little too black? If one of these is the case, mix a small amount of the opposite colour with some 50/50 polish and methylated spirit and add this to the mixture. Apply another one or two rubbers and do the same again, ie, leave the work for a while and then, when you return, take note of your first impressions.

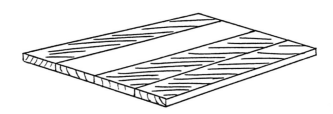

Fig. 29 *An example of a table top where one board is lighter than the others.*

Once the colour has been adjusted, the process can then continue until the odd board is a good match to the others. Be careful not to make it too dark; if anything a colour correction such as this is better a little on the light side.

Whenever carrying out a colouring or touching-up procedure, the piece of furniture being worked upon should, as far as practical, be in its normal everyday position. For example, if it is a chest of drawers it should be standing on the floor with its drawers in place. It is important to move around and view the piece from different directions and, if possible, occasionally rotate it so that the main light source is coming from a different angle. The reason for this is that many woods appear either lighter or darker depending upon the position from which they are viewed and also upon the angle that the light source makes with the surface. You may find that a piece of wood which looked a lot lighter than others from one direction is less outstanding or even the opposite when seen from another direction, so a compromise has to be reached.

Whilst on the subject of light, it is particularly important where colouring is concerned (as with stain testing on page 34) to do the work near a window in order to use as much daylight as possible. Artificial light will give a false impression of colour.

A further point: the result of applying a number of colour rubbers to a part of the surface means that the coloured area has received more polish than the rest. This should be balanced up by applying the same amount of rubbers of ordinary polish to the other areas. This must, obviously, be the same dilution as the colour, ie. 50/50 polish/methylated spirit.

The second situation that we can look at is a drawer front, Fig. 30, where a piece of veneer has been made to replace a missing one. Even though it has been stained, it is still found to be a little light after the first few rubbers of polish have been applied. Owing to the shape of the area it would be very difficult to apply an even colour

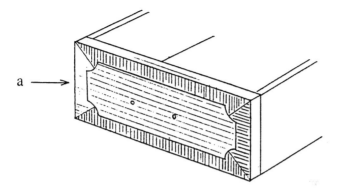

Fig. 30 *A replacement piece of veneer that requires additional colouring. (a)*

with a rubber, so this is an ideal case for a brush. The general procedure is exactly the same as above, ie. apply some colour, leave it for a while, examine it and then correct the mix if necessary.

The skill is in the coating. It should be done quickly, but carefully and accurately, making sure that there are no runs and that the colour, as mentioned on page 63, does not overlap onto the darker areas.

Touching-up and colour matching is quite an art in itself and a little practice is needed in order to do this successfully.

Surplus colour mixtures can be stored in air tight jars, which must be clean and dry and labelled, ie. "Strong medium colour", "Medium reddish colour", etc.

After the touching-up and colouring have been finished, two rubbers of polish are applied to seal in the colouring, and also build up the surface a little further ready for bodying-up.

Before leaving this section, a few words on "earth pigments" may be useful. These are fine powders available in a range of different colours. They can be mixed with french polish to make a sort of french polish-based paint. I do not know where the name originates, but this is known in the trade as a "dope". The colours normally available include Yellow Ochre, Brown Umber, Orange Chrome, Canary Yellow, and Titanium White.

The use of a dope can, as an example, help to hide an unsightly area of damage such as a cigarette burn. A small amount of the appropriate colours are mixed together with a little french polish to match the colour of the surrounding wood, and carefully applied with a pencil brush using one of the basic touching-up techniques (strokes or dots). Spirit colours can also be added to adjust the colour if necessary. The polish used to produce the mixture should be fairly thin, say two parts polish to one part methylated spirit.

Another example of the use of dope is around the edges of plywood. Plywood has been used quite extensively in mass production furniture over the years. One of its disadvantages, however, is that the striped edges of the laminations tend to look unsightly, and it is common practice to cover these with a dope that matches the main surface.

After applying dope, french polishing is then continued in the normal way.

6

WAX POLISHING

After the french polishing has been finished and left to harden for three to four days, extra protection can be given by wax polishing. But first let us look at the surface which at this point will be quite shiny. This is referred to by some people as the "toffee apple" stage. Obviously, if you want a high-gloss finish, this is fine and you can continue to wax polish or even burnish the surface for a higher shine still (Page 86). You may, on the other hand, prefer the shine to be reduced a little to what I call a "mellow sheen", and in this case a further operation is required which is called "cutting-back". This is achieved by gently rubbing the surface with very fine steel wool (grade 0000) dipped in wax polish as a lubricant. The procedure must be done very carefully and the steel wool must be kept moistened by the wax, otherwise it will scratch the surface. The strokes must be straight with the grain and not curved, and every square inch must receive the same amount of work and pressure. Instead of actually dipping the steel wool straight into the wax polish tin, it is best to take a lump of wax out and put it on a piece of cardboard or something similar. A soft wax polish should be used for this operation, and it is best to use a fairly dark coloured one with the exception, of course, of a light piece of work. The dark wax polish will find its way into small nooks and crannies that may show up light if a paler polish is used. Do no more than a couple of square feet at a time and polish off with a clean soft cloth. It is usually necessary to cut back twice in order to make sure that all of the surface is covered evenly. Following this, the piece of work can then be wax polished in the conventional way a few times in order to add a little extra protection. If you have time to do this 4-5 times, all the better, and this can be done with an ordinary light polish. The dark polish need only be used for the first one or two applications, (ie. the cutting back). The best method I have found for wax polishing quickly and successfully is to use three cloths. A 'putting on' cloth, a 'first polishing cloth' and then a 'second polishing cloth' to finish off. The polish should be put on in circles, straightened off, left to dry for about five minutes and then polished off with the first cloth, followed straight away by the second one. The advantage of this method is that the second polishing cloth is kept nice and clean, which helps to make this final buffing much easier. Lay the materials out on clean newspaper in order to avoid picking up dust etc, and make sure that your polishing cloths are perfectly clean. It is a good idea to keep them separately in small plastic bags.

Careful choice of wax polish is important. Some contain very strong solvents that can affect the surface of a recently polished piece of work. Always use simple white spirit or turpentine-based wax polishes.

An additional point on hardness: although a french polished finish is quite hard after a few days, it takes about a fortnight for it to cure fully. It is as well, therefore, particularly where table tops are concerned, to allow this period of time before putting them into use. Even the weight of a lace decoration can cause an imprint if left on the surface before full hardening is complete.

So the job is finished. A further wax polishing once every six months will keep it looking good and also maintain a level of protection.

One final word. As mentioned earlier, please practise only on scrap pieces of wood and inexpensive furniture. If the piece of furniture that needs attention is likely to have any value, whether monetary or sentimental, seek advice first. Most restorers, being interested in their work, will be only too willing to offer advice. If they are good enough to do this, please do not keep them talking for too long. Remember, they have to make a living!

7

CLEANING PRIOR TO RE-POLISHING

If the existing finish on a piece of furniture is dull and wax polishing will not revive it, it is possible that cleaning and re-french polishing may be necessary to restore its appearance.

To enable the new finish to adhere properly, the surface must be perfectly clean and free from wax and grease, which means cleaning off the wax polish that has accumulated over the years. To do this, the surface is moistened with a cloth containing white spirit and gently rubbed with very fine steel wool (0000 grade). Turpentine substitute is not quite as good for this purpose as it is a lower grade product, and pure turpentine tends to be a little oily.

This process may have to be repeated two or three times. Do not attempt too large an area at once. About one square foot is a comfortable size. A small piece of polisher's wadding is ideal for applying the white spirit. Only use the steel wool whilst the surface is moist. If it dries up, re-wet it. When you think the surface is clean, wet it again, wipe it with a piece of clean cloth and then examine the cloth. If it has become dirty, there is obviously still more grime to be removed. Change the steel wool frequently. It is wise to wear gloves for this operation as spirits and solvents such as these can affect the skin. Disposable vinyl gloves are useful for this purpose and will last a reasonable amount of time.

Methylated spirit should not be used as a cleaning agent on french polished surfaces as it will soften and remove the polish. It is useful, however, for cleaning small items that have been previously finished with either varnish or a cellulose-type lacquer as it will not soften these. This work must be done quite fast as methylated spirit evaporates very quickly. Moisten a small piece of cloth and gently rub the surface a little at a time. The scouring action of the cloth may be sufficient to remove the grime on its own, otherwise a piece of very fine steel wool (0000 grade) may help. I must emphasise that this should only be carried out on very small areas and preferably out of doors. The vapour from methylated spirit can be harmful and is also flammable. Always allow adequate ventilation even when using small amounts.

If in doubt about the type of finish, test a small area with methylated spirit in an inconspicuous place. If it starts to soften and goes tacky it is very likely french polish and should be cleaned with white spirit. Otherwise it is almost certain to be either a varnish or a synthetic lacquer.

Whilst thinking about safety and cleaning, do bear in mind that white spirit is also a flammable liquid and, although it does not vaporise quite as quickly as methylated spirit, it can be harmful in an enclosed space.

For both of these materials and any others that contain solvents, careful use, handling and storage are extremely important along with ample ventilation.

Polished surfaces can be cleaned by other means such as hot water containing a small amount of either washing soda or household ammonia. The problem with using water is that in many cases it can be detrimental to the piece of furniture concerned. If there are cracks, the water may seep underneath the polish and the presence of either soda or ammonia will cause a darkening of the wood. Furthermore, it is inadvisable to use water on veneered surfaces as it could soften the glue and cause the veneer to lift.

The above methods describe the use of easily obtainable materials. There are, of course, proprietary branded cleaning products available. Some are more searching than white spirit and will remove grime very quickly, but one must take care. Being strong solvents, there is always the possibility that the surface finish itself may be softened and removed inadvertently.

Before carrying out any cleaning operation, it is always wise to do a small test in an unnoticeable place to make sure that you are removing the grime only and not the finish itself.

Do bear in mind that where antique furniture is concerned, the dark shading in corners etc. that has built up over the years is very much a part of the character of that piece of furniture and should not be removed. Therefore, cleaning must be carried out very carefully in order to take off only the unwanted grime and not the "history".

After the cleaning has been finished and then put aside to dry overnight, the surface can be lightly sanded all over with grade 320 paper, being very careful, of course, not to sand the corners (page 27 & photograph opposite page 48). The purpose here is twofold: firstly, as an addition to the cleaning process to make sure that the surface of the old polish is completely exposed and, secondly, to abrade the surface a little in order to form a mechanical key for the new material. This is particularly important where the previous finish is a varnish or a cellulose-based lacquer. When re-polishing on top of an existing french polished finish, the methylated spirit in the new material will slightly soften the existing surface, which helps to provide a good bond. However, as methylated spirit does not soften varnishes or cellulose, the bond is not quite as good and it is therefore essential to provide a clean sanded surface in an attempt to gain as much mechanical adhesion as possible. If the surface has not been cleaned well enough, and there is perhaps a residue of wax polish left, the new finish will not adhere properly. This shows up as a "fuzzing" on the surface and is known as a "tearing-up". When this happens, the first rubber usually goes on quite well and the tearing-up occurs on the second or third rubbers. The only real solution is to carefully take off the new polish with methylated spirit and then re-clean the surface. If polishing is continued, the fuzzing will sometimes flatten down and disappear, but this is not an ideal situation. The area where the tearing-up occurred will, due to its low adhesion, probably be prone to scratching easily.

8

STRIPPING OFF OLD FINISHES

I know I am repeating myself here, but do please make sure that this is the last resort! For some years now, the best material for this purpose has been, and still is, paint remover. Paint removers are strong chemical products and as such must be treated with the greatest caution. Some of the chemicals used in these products are not only dangerous by inhalation, but can also be absorbed through the skin. It is essential, therefore, that stripping should be done out of doors, preferably with a slight breeze. Always wear goggles and always wear gloves. (Never mind what the neighbours think!).

There are several makes of paint remover on the market, but probably the most popular one in this country is "Nitro-Mors". From this manufacturer there are a number of different types for different applications, but the one that I find most suitable for general use is packaged in a green container and is termed "water washable". Do not be misled, this does not mean that the surface must be washed with water and that you cannot use white spirit or methylated spirit. This material has a fairly thick consistency which makes it a little easier to use than thinner products of a similar type.

Apart from safety equipment, the following items are needed :

a few old newspapers;   a $1^1/_2$" paint brush;   a screw top jam jar; a blunt paint scraper;   some old rags;   a pack of grade 4 steel wool; and a pair of old scissors for cutting the steel wool.

Before starting, make sure that you can get to running water quickly, just in case of emergencies. As mentioned above, goggles are essential, as accidents do happen. They provide much better protection against chemicals than safety spectacles. It is very important when using commercial chemicals, such as paint removers, to follow the manufacturer's safety instructions to the letter. I can remember a nasty little incident some time ago when a small amount of paint remover found its way past a pair of safety spectacles that I was wearing at the time. I can confirm, without any doubt, that the pain is excruciating even if the most minute amount gets into your eyes. If this ever happens, keep calm, go to a tap and rinse with lots of water. Obviously, it is wise to obtain medical advice afterwards.

If there is not a tap near the work area, fill a bucket with water and keep this close by. Contact with the skin will also cause a stinging sensation and a damp cloth kept handy is a useful precaution.

In the list on the previous page I have included a blunt scraper. This can be an ordinary flat paint scraper, Fig. 31. The edges and corners, however, must be sandpapered well in order to remove any sharpness that might scratch the surface of the wood.

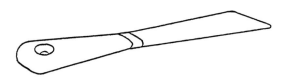

Fig. 31 *An ordinary paint scraper can be used, but the sharp edges must be removed.*

Pour a small amount of paint remover into the jar and cut two pieces of steel wool 4"- 5" long. Mould each piece of steel wool into a small pad and put them aside ready for use.

Using the brush, apply a liberal coat of paint remover to the surface. It is best to work on an area of about one square foot at a time. Leave this first coat to soak in for 3-4 minutes. Next apply another coat on top of the first, but this one should be left to soak a little longer, perhaps 10 minutes, and then apply a third coat on top of the second. Leave all of this for a further 15 minutes and then, pushing the paint scraper forward, lift off the softened material. The consistency of this will vary depending upon the type of finish and also its thickness. If it is very runny, the number of coats can be reduced, and on the next section try two instead of three. The softened material should be scraped onto a piece of newspaper and then disposed of. After the bulk of the old finish has been removed in this way, coat up the area again, leave for 4-5 minutes and rub in the direction of the grain with the first piece of steel wool. This will usually pick up quite a lot of material. After going over the surface with this first piece of steel wool, take the second one and continue until the surface is dry. The above operation of coating up and using steel wool should be repeated three times, or until you are satisfied that the surface is perfectly clean. Once you have assured yourself that this is so, repeat the operation once more to be absolutely sure!

When using coarse steel wool, make sure your fingers are wrapped around the outside of the pad and not caught through a loop. It can be extremely sharp and accidents have been caused in this way. Work in the direction of the grain of the wood as far as possible. If there are places where working across the grain is unavoidable, use a steel wool of a finer grade.

It is not always practical to use a scraper on curved and moulded surfaces. In such cases it is often necessary to use steel wool all the way through. Obviously, during the first stages it will become clogged quite quickly, so it is as well to have some extra pieces cut ready for use.

Corners and crevices can be cleaned out with a blunt scraper. A small hardwood stick, sharpened flat at one end is very useful for this purpose.

When the first piece of steel wool becomes clogged-up, replace it with the second one, and then cut a further piece to replace this, and so on.

Paint removers contain waxes to prevent them from evaporating too quickly. Traces of these will be left on the surface, and so, after stripping, a thorough cleaning with white spirit should be carried out. At the same time, a light rub with steel wool will further clean the surface. Apply the white spirit to about one square foot at a time, rub lightly with the steel wool (grade 4) and wipe off with a clean cloth. After this has been left to dry (preferably overnight), a wipe over with methylated spirit is worthwhile as a final cleansing. Following this, a light sanding with 320 grade paper will complete the job, and the surface is then ready for the first stages of polishing.

Part Stripping

Please bear in mind where stripping is concerned that it is not always necessary to strip the whole of a piece of furniture. In fact, part stripping is often desirable in order to retain as much of the original finish as possible. An example of this is where the leg of a table may have suffered extensive heat damage. In this sort of case it is quite in order to strip the damaged section on its own, and then stain and re-polish this to match the rest of the frame. The most common example of this is, of course, where a table top is in need of stripping, but the remainder of the table is in good condition and only requires cleaning and re-polishing, or indeed sometimes only wax polishing.

In addition to retaining the original finish there is the obvious advantage of saving time and materials. However, it is very important that the staining and colouring is done carefully if the work is to match well with the existing surfaces.

STRIPPING TANKS

I think perhaps I ought to say a few words about stripping tanks. This method of stripping off old finishes has become very popular during the past few years, largely due to the fact that stripped pine furniture and doors have been very much in vogue.

I can't say that I agree with this method, as it can be quite detrimental to both the wood and the piece of furniture itself. The process seems to leach out the resins and oils from the surface, causing it to dry out and crack. Also, if the item concerned is left in the tank for too long, it is likely that the glue will be dissolved and the joints weakened. I would certainly not recommend the dipping of furniture, but I suppose there is a case for things such as pine doors. The reason I offer this exception is that to remove by hand the numerous layers of paint that have accumulated over the years is, to say the least, a daunting prospect for anyone.

There are quite a few companies that do this sort of work nowadays. It is well worth trying to find someone who has had some previous experience of those in your locality, as advice and recommendation are always worth having.

9

FURTHER NOTES AND TECHNIQUES

EBONIZING

In its basic sense, this is black french polishing, first using a black stain, followed by black or very dark grain-filler and then followed by black polish.

To imitate polished ebony, which is a very fine-grained wood, a full finish must be produced. It is wise, particularly if the wood being polished is fairly open-grained, to apply more than one application of grainfiller. For ebonizing, grainfilling can be carried out on the bare wood. Black polish may be purchased or, alternatively, made up by adding spirit black to ordinary polish. If the latter is contemplated, remember that spirit black is a blue-black, and the addition of just a tiny amount of red and possibly a little yellow may be necessary to soften its appearance. Black isn't just black. There are different tones ranging from blue-black to brown-black. Ebony is approximately in the middle and the addition of these colours will neutralise the blue that is present in the spirit black. Spirit black, in either powder or concentrate form, is very strong. An approximate guide to mixing for half a litre of french polish would be either two 5ml teaspoons of powder or six tablespoons (120ml) of concentrate.

GRAINFILLING

This is a method of speeding up the polishing process, which is helpful if you have large areas to do, but it has the disadvantage that on some woods it can dull the appearance of the grain and figuring. Because of this it is always wise to do a polished test piece first, to make sure that the right colour grainfiller has been selected. There is a certain amount of confusion over whether grainfiller should be applied to the bare wood or to the surface after it has been stained and sealed with a few rubbers of polish. I personally prefer the latter, as there is less chance of altering the appearance of the wood by the grainfiller being absorbed too much into the finer pores. When this happens the result is a sort of faint "muddiness", and a few rubbers of polish first help to prevent this occurring.

Another problem that can occur is that of grainfiller looking too light in the grain. The colour chosen should be slightly darker than the required **finished** colour of the work, and **not** the natural colour of the wood.

Grainfiller is a paste material that is rubbed into the grain in circles with a small piece of coarse hessian. It should be applied to no more than approximately one square foot at a time, and then the surplus rubbed off immediately with a larger piece of the same material. Rub off hard across the grain and then straight with the grain to finish. The reason for working on only a small area at a time, is to make absolutely sure that all the excess material has been rubbed off before it starts to dry. Even when this is done there is still the possibility of a slight film being left on the surface. This can cause adhesion problems between the successive layers of polish and the previous ones. To help prevent this, wipe the surface over with a cloth moistened (not wet) with white spirit about fifteen minutes after applying the grainfiller. This does not, as you may think, remove the material from the grain, at least not to any degree. After this has been done the piece of work should be left overnight to harden and then the surface can be eased down (very lightly sanded) with 400 grade paper. Be careful not to sand through the polish and stain and cause patches. Following this, I always wipe the surface with a moist methylated spirit cloth. This, however, should only be done once otherwise the thin layer of polish previously applied could be softened and removed. The purpose of easing down and wiping with methylated spirit is to further make sure that all traces of surplus material have been removed, so that the subsequent applications of polish will adhere properly. The object of the exercise, of course, is to leave the grainfiller in the pores of the wood, not on the surface.

Being a paste, the grainfiller will collect in corners, crevices and mouldings. A sharpened stick should be used to clean these out. Fig. 32.

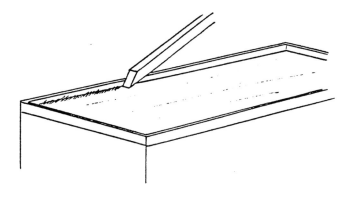

Fig. 32 *A sharpened stick being used to remove grainfiller from crevices and mouldings.*

Standard colours are oak, mahogany and walnut, and these are usually obtainable in light, medium and dark. Natural is also available. This is a creamy colour and is useful for very light woods. Grainfiller should be stirred well before and during use. If it is too thick, it will be difficult to use and should be thinned with white spirit to the consistency of medium custard.

It is best to leave the initial layers of polish to harden for a few hours before grainfilling is carried out. I have not been able to substantiate this, but I believe that if it is carried out too soon, the oils and solvents present may reduce the ultimate hardness of the polish.

Grainfilling is a fairly messy job and I would strongly recommend the use of disposable gloves.

BURNISHING

In Chapter 6 I described the process of cutting back the finish with wax polish and fine steel wool in order to reduce the shine a little. On occasions, however, it is desirable to produce a finish that does have a glass-like appearance. This may be to suit a particular piece of furniture that was originally finished in this manner.

The method is quite simple but, as with most things, a little care is necessary. After the work has been left to harden for a few days (a week if possible), instead of being cut back, the surface is burnished with a very fine abrasive in order to polish it even further. Special burnishing creams are available, but, if it is a small area that does not warrant the expense, a metal polish such as Brasso can be used as an alternative. There is a snag with burnishing, however, which is that the polished surface being worked upon must have a full finish, otherwise the burnishing cream will get into the open pores and show up white when it dries out.

Apply the material with a soft cloth, and work in the direction of the grain with a moderate pressure, keeping the cloth moist by adding more, a little at a time. Work gradually over the whole surface, and polish off using two pieces of cloth as with wax polishing, the first one to remove the surplus and the second for a final buffing. Repeat this two or three times to make sure that the surface has been burnished evenly all over.

Make sure that the entire surface is free from dust and that polishing cloths are soft and clean. The smallest amount of dust or grit could be disastrous.

To finish off, it is wise to wax polish two or three times to give a little extra protection.

The main problem with a full burnished finish is that a higher shine is produced, which means that imperfections on the surface will show up all the more. Owing to this, not only must the quality of the french polishing be of a very high standard, but the surface of the wood must be in first class condition before you start.

As a point of interest, the ultimate acid finish that is used on pianos, as well as removing the oil, is also a form of burnishing. A little advanced for this book, but in principle fine Vienna chalk is sprinkled on the surface, followed by a very weak solution of sulphuric acid. These are rubbed together over the surface. The oil is absorbed and the resulting paste lightly burnishes the finish.

DULLING and MATTING DOWN

If we look back at the later stages of polishing, after the finish has been left to harden for a few days, the surface is cut back using wax polish and fine steel wool, which reduces the level of brightness and provides a more mellow appearance. Dulling and matting are merely extensions of this same principle, but instead of wax polish and steel wool, fine abrasive powders are used as a way of either reducing or removing the shine further. Generally speaking, partial removal of the shine to a satin-type sheen is referred to as dulling, and a total reduction of shine is referred to as a matt finish.

The abrasive normally used for this purpose is fine pumice powder. Rottenstone, which is very fine and really a burnishing powder, is also used, but to raise the shine as opposed to lowering it. (This will be explained shortly.)

There are two methods of application, the first being a dry one using a brush to apply the powder, and the second using either water or oil as a lubricant. Water should be avoided on french polished surfaces unless the finish has had several weeks to harden. For our purposes oil is the most suitable and can be used after three or four days.

The choice of which abrasive and method depends on the degree of shine reduction required. This is perhaps best divided into three levels. First of all, for a small reduction, the surface can be gently brushed with fine pumice powder. The pumice should be sprinkled on the surface and then brushed lightly in the direction of the grain. A clean dry shoe brush or clothes brush can be used for this purpose. It should, however, be fairly soft and it is wise to keep it specially for use as a "dulling brush". Corners, mouldings and carvings are best dealt with using a small paint brush. The secret is to gently brush everything by the same amount so that the reduction is even all over. Very lightly, two or three times is the best method. Sprinkling the powder onto the surface is traditionally done by placing a small amount inside a piece of open weave cloth, which is drawn up at the top, and held with a piece of string or an elastic band. This is called a "pounce bag" and as it is tapped on the surface the powder slowly seeps through the cloth. A sugar shaker, the type used for cooking, can also be used, and is best for the following method where oil is applied first.

The next level of reduction is achieved by rubbing the surface first with fine pumice powder and oil. This will actually dull the surface more than we need for a satin finish, and so following this a little shine is then brought back using rottenstone. White oil is ideal for this sort of work. Spread the oil liberally on two to three square feet at a time. Shake the pumice powder on top of it and rub with a folded pad of soft cloth that has been moistened with a little of the oil. Continue gently two or three times over the whole surface. Following this, clean the surface with white spirit and then repeat the operation using the rottenstone and a fresh piece of cloth. This will polish the surface a little and the result will be a satin finish. Instead of a cloth pad, a small piece of thick felt can be used for this purpose. If the surface is still duller than required, one or two applications of wax polish will also raise the shine further.

The last level of reduction is a full matt finish and this is quite simply a repeat of the above process but without bringing up the shine afterwards.

After the dulling has been completed to the level required the surface should be cleaned, first using white spirit and then vinegar. It is best to leave an hour or so in between to allow the white spirit to dry off properly. Apply the white spirit to two to three square feet at a time with a moist cloth, rub gently, and then dry off with another clean, soft cloth. The vinegar is a final cleansing and will remove any remaining smears that may be left behind.

Work using fine powders can be a little dusty, so it is wise to wear a dust mask for this type of process.

On page 139 I have included a table that will provide a quick reference to these methods.

Do remember that, as with burnishing, the surface must be left to harden for a few days before this sort of work is carried out.

FURTHER RUBBERING TECHNIQUES

As an extension to the basic methods of using the rubber, the following section consists of useful techniques that will help towards achieving a good standard of work.

Re-Starting

Whenever a piece of work is left, whether it is for a couple of hours or a few days or so, upon re-starting, always ease down lightly with 400 grade paper, dust and apply one rubber of polish. This will ensure that the work is smooth, dust-free and ready for the next part of the process. The addition of one or two extra rubbers as such will make very little difference to the overall finish.

Runs and Thickened Edges

Runs are our arch enemy. The reason for this is that they are almost impossible to remove without damaging the surface that has already been applied. Once the polish has hardened, the only thing you can do, is try to level the run down with a piece of fine sandpaper, using a little oil as a lubricant. However, what usually happens when doing this, is that the surrounding polish is also removed along with the stain underneath and the result is a horrible mess. This area has then to be re-stained which seldom blends in perfectly. In addition to this, the polish has to be made good and usually the fullness of the repair ends up different compared with the rest of the work. At this point, after tearing your hair out, you are thinking to yourself, "Would it have been better to have left the run alone in the first place?" Obviously, had it been very small and in an inconspicuous place this may well have been the best policy. Runs are the last thing you want to see on a piece of finished work, and the best course by far is to avoid producing them in the first place. This, in itself, is all part of the skill of the subject! It is essential to watch the rubber all the time and be aware of where the polish is being placed.   Along with runs, thickened edges and corners must also be avoided as they can be just as unsightly, particularly to the trained eye. With this in mind, we will go on to look at a few causes of such things in the hope of avoiding them.

The main cause of runs is when the rubber is inadvertently either pulled or pushed across an edge as shown in Fig. 33.

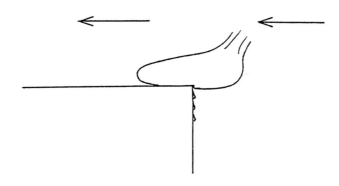

Fig. 33 *Rubber being pulled (or pushed) across an edge.*
Runs are inevitable.

When the rubber is brought down to land on the surface it should always land a little way in from the edge (Fig. 19, page 46), otherwise the scraping action of the corner will cause the polish to run down the vertical face.   When leaving the work it is quite in order to "run off" an edge as there is not a risk of causing runs in this way. The golden rule to remember is that you can always go off at an edge but never on to an edge.

A cause that may not be immediately apparent is shown in Fig. 34. This often occurs when working flat surfaces like table tops. As the rubber runs along the edges, if it is not perfectly parallel, it will, to a small degree, be pulled over the edge and runs will be produced.

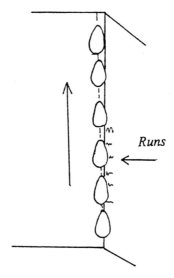

Fig. 34
Runs will develop if the course of the rubber is not parallel to the edge of the work.

Runs

Obviously, on the side where you are standing they will be seen and can be quickly mopped up with the rubber, but on the edge away from you the runs may not be noticed.

Thickened Edges
Thickened edges are generally produced by either the rubber being too wet or overhanging too much as it is run along the edge of a piece of work. Fig. 35.
A small amount of polish is deposited along the corner and if unnoticed will eventually build up to form a thick edge. Not only is this unsightly, but it is also very bad practice.

Fig. 35 *Too much overhang and excessive pressure will cause thickened edges (a).*

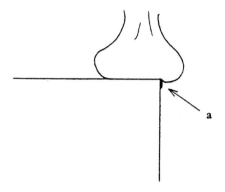

Often, when working on a piece of furniture there will be a number of surfaces that are out of view. The best thing to do is to run your fingers around these edges after each sequence with the rubber. By doing this any wetness such as runs or edge build-up will be detected and can be dealt with straight away.

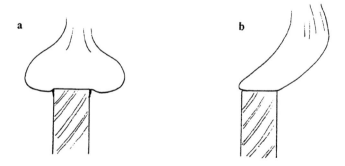

Fig. 36 *A rubber that is too large can also cause thickened edges on narrow surfaces (a). It is best to use either the tip of the rubber (b), or a smaller one.*

Another common cause of edge build-up is when polishing a narrow surface such as the edge of a shelf. If the rubber is too large excessive polish will be deposited along each side, Fig. 36a.

It is best to use just the tip of the rubber, Fig. 36b, or alternatively make up a small separate rubber especially for use on the edges.

The Perimeter

For some reason, when bodying-up a flat surface, the perimeter of the work never seems to build quite as well as the middle. It is, therefore, necessary to work a few extra sets of small circles around the edge to compensate for this. Perhaps one set for every three sequences of ordinary circles. There is an old saying: "Look after the edges and the middle will look after itself."

This is only a rough guide; it is well to monitor the fullness as the work progresses. If the perimeter becomes too full, stop the extra circles. If not full enough, increase them. The object, after all, is to end up with an even fullness over the entire surface.

This also applies when working on a panel inside a frame, but in this case a smaller rubber may be needed in order to be able to work right into the corners.

Keep Moving

I know that I am repeating myself here, but just a reminder. The rubber must never be stationary on the surface, not even for a split second, otherwise there is a risk of sticking and tearing the soft polish. I said on page 49 that once the oil is present on the surface there is no longer a risk of sticking, and this is so, providing the rubber is always moving. This is also important when the rubber lands, and again when it leaves the surface. Fig. 19, page 46.

Working Inside a Frame

On page 45, I described the aircraft carrier technique of landing, running along and leaving the surface. This is obviously fine where the surface is flat, but when it is surrounded by either a frame or a moulding, a different procedure is necessary. This is carried out in two stages. First, the tip of the rubber is run up and down each side, close to the moulding. After this has been done, the rubber can then be worked lengthways. At the end of each run along the panel, its direction is turned, ready to start the next run going the opposite way, as shown in Fig. 37.

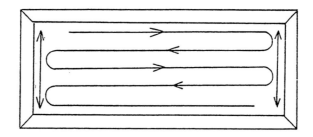

Fig. 37 *On a small panel run along each end before working lengthways.*

The long runs must blend in with the cross strokes at each end while the polish is still moist, otherwise, if it has dried, the result will be a double layer which will eventually produce an uneven surface. To achieve this on large panels it is best to divide the width up into several sections. Fig. 38.

When working along the inside edge of the frame or moulding, use the tip of the rubber and make sure that it is pressed well into the corner. (Photograph opposite page 64)

On small items that are surrounded by a moulding or a raised edge, such as drawer fronts, it is often best to run around all four

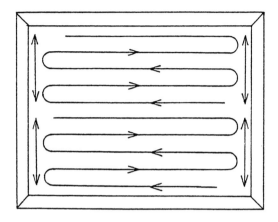

Fig. 38 *On a larger panel work in sections.*

edges first, working in and out of the corners. As the rubber approaches each corner, it must be turned so that its tip is pointing out towards the moulding as it changes direction.

Turned Work

Most turned work can be dealt with using a rubber. However, brushes are often used to save time, particularly when the turnings are complicated. This may be all very well in skilled hands and where the brush is only used for the base coats, but I strongly believe that it is best to use the rubber as much as possible in order to maintain a quality of finish. Having said this, there are, of course, situations where the turning, or part of the turning, concerned will be too fine for a rubber to be used, and where it becomes necessary to use a small brush. In such cases, it is important to apply only one or two light coats, as fine detail on turned work can easily become clogged with polish, which will spoil the appearance.

Fig. 39 is a drawing of a typical turned table leg and the arrows give an indication of the path of the rubber.

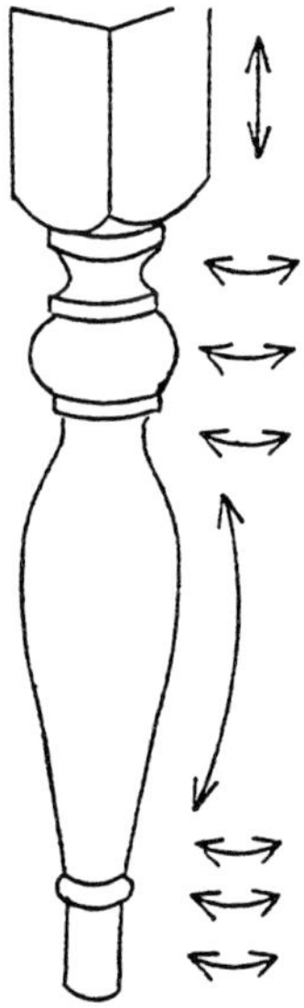

Fig. 39
Work down from the top,
one section at a time.

This is really quite a quick procedure despite the number of arrows. Most of the work is done with the tip of a small rubber. The action of pushing the rubber into these various shapes means that it will need re-shaping fairly regularly. It is a good idea, therefore, to practise this so that it can be done quite quickly. When working on such things as a chair or the base of a table, I always find it best to work from the inside out. The piece of furniture concerned must be at a convenient height so that you can put your head inside the frame in order to be able to see the part you are working on properly. This is very important. If you try to polish areas that you cannot see, it is almost certain that either runs or inferior work will result. On such a leg as shown in Fig. 39, once the square section has been done at the top, you then, with the tip of the rubber, start working around the turning. Each section must be completed all the way round before working down to the next one and so on. The starting point for each section should be from the inside of the frame and slightly further than half way round. In Fig. 40 I have marked the approximate starting point with the letter S.

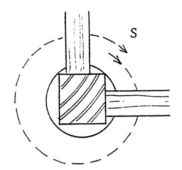

Fig. 40
Always start from inside the frame.

Start from this position, bring the rubber around to the front and lift it off. Repeat this on the opposite side. Finish off by overlapping a little at the front, and remember when lifting the rubber off the surface it must be moving. After a little practice you will find it possible in many cases to work all the way round in one operation, finishing off at the rear. This is slightly better as it reduces the chances of double coating at the front.

Move down to the next section and do the same again. This may seem a little involved, but once again, like a lot of the techniques we use, the time taken is very small.

The above method is used when applying the initial rubbers of polish, and also during the finishing off stages. When there is oil present and bodying-up is in progress, the rubber is shuffled backwards and forwards around each part of the turning. This "shuffling" action is the same as that described on page 57 for working on narrow surfaces. One sequence of shuffling around each section will be roughly equal to one set of circles on a flat surface.

Carvings

We can divide carving roughly into four types -

1. Shallow surface carving, usually in the form of geometric patterns, popular during the sixteenth century and also thus on reproduction furniture of this period.
2. Shallow relief carving of such things as leaves, flowers and scrolls.
3. Deep decorative carving.
4. Artistic and figure carving, which can include the full or partial carving of almost anything.

1. Shallow Surface Carving

The first type, shallow surface carving, consists of patterns and shapes cut lightly into the surface. This sort of work should only be polished very lightly, just enough to give the main surface a sheen. It is best to keep the polish out of the fine channels of the carving altogether. Use the rubber as dry as possible. If it is too wet the channels will fill up and the overall effect will be spoilt. After the surface has been polished a little in this way, leave it to harden and then bring up the sheen by wax polishing several times, using a soft brush to polish off over the decorated areas.

2. Shallow Relief Carving

This sort of decorative work is found on many pieces of furniture and can consist of floral designs, leaves, scrolls etc. It is usually either cut into, or stands slightly proud above, the surface. An example of this is the type of decoration often found on the tops of cabriole chair legs that follow the style of the Georgian period. Fig. 41.

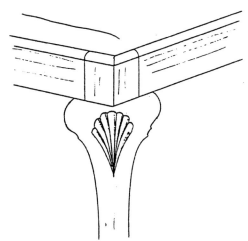

Fig. 41
Shallow relief carving.
Shown here on a chair leg.

The outer surfaces of this sort of decoration are usually polished to the same level as the rest of the work, using the tip of the rubber. There are sometimes fairly deep areas, particularly where scrolls are concerned. It is unwise to bring up too much shine in these places and two thin coats of polish with a fine brush is usually sufficient. A light sheen can then be brought up by wax polishing when the whole piece has been finished.

3. *Deep Decorative Carving*
The subject of this type of work is infinitely variable: floral designs, semi-relief carving of figures, animals, people etc.

Very often found on furniture in the form of plaques or panels. In general, it should not be polished, as the production of a shine could very well ruin the character produced by the original artist. If the carving is very dirty, clean it carefully using white spirit and soft brushes. Strips of soft cloth wrapped around the end of a small stick are also very useful. Do not, under any circumstances, use a metal object or (perish the thought) a wire brush. Great care must obviously be taken not to break off any of the pieces. After cleaning, leave to dry thoroughly and then carefully wax polish several times to protect the surface from further grime.

4. *Artistic and Figure Carving*
     This can include almost any subject that has been carved by an artistic craftsman. Examples include lifelike figures of people, animals, birds, fruit etc. that have been produced three dimensionally.
     As with the case above, this sort of fine artistic work should never be brought up to a shine, unless it is clear that the original artist intended this. In general, it should receive the same treatment as above, a careful cleaning and wax polishing. The original treatment by the artist may be difficult to determine; some wax polish their sculptures, some use linseed oil and, indeed, there are also those who insist on leaving the wood in its natural state. The problem, of course, with this is that if a piece of wood is left un-sealed, it allows the ingress of dust and grime.

Pierced Work
     Pierced work is where a shape, a slot or a pattern is cut out of a flat piece of wood. The back splat of a Chippendale style chair is a typical example. Fig. 42. Fretwork, as a point of interest, is an example of fine pierced work.
     The outer flat surfaces must be worked as dry as possible to prevent polish forming "thickened edges" inside the pierced shapes (page 91). Whilst you are working with the rubber, you must

constantly run your fingers around the holes to make sure that there are no runs or wet patches.

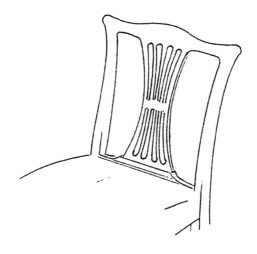

Fig. 42 *Pierced work on the back splat of a chair.*

Treatment on the inside edges is quite straightforward. If the holes are large enough, the tip of a small rubber can be used, otherwise a small soft brush. One or two coats or rubbers is all that is normally necessary. Leave the rest to wax polish. Too much shine on the inside of piercing should be avoided. When working on these inside edges make sure that there are no runs on the flat surfaces (front and back). If found, rub off quickly with your hand.

Fine Reeding and Mouldings

It is not always possible to use a rubber on intricate shaped work. There are sometimes nooks and crannies that you just cannot reach, even with the tip of the smallest rubber. Having said this, a brush should only be used as a last resort. It is all about quality. A rubber will produce a better finish.

Framed Mirrors and Glass Doors

The best method of keeping polish etc. off the glass is to use masking tape (not sellotape). Obviously, it must be cut to length and placed in position accurately. Once in position, rub your fingers over the tape several times to make sure that it has adhered properly all over. It is amazing how easily polish and stain can creep underneath. Never leave it on for more than one day. Over a period of time it sticks faster to the surface and becomes very difficult to remove, sometimes leaving part of the adhesive behind which then has to be cleaned off with white spirits. If it is a new mirror that you are polishing, remember that the inside edge of the frame that touches the glass must be coated with matt black before the mirror is assembled. Matt black paint is best for this purpose, but, if not available, spirit black mixed with french polish will make a good substitute.

Working up to a Joint

Joint lines are to be found on most pieces of work where one piece of wood meets another. This could be a framework such as that shown in Fig. 43.

Always start with the innermost pieces and work outwards. On this example we would start with the short pieces *a*, then the cross rails *b*, and finally the upright pieces at each end *c*. Work up to the joints as accurately as possible trying not to overlap.

Another example is a dining chair and a good system is shown in Fig. 44. Once again work from the middle outwards. Start with *a*, the centre part of the back, and then do the bottom stretcher *b*. This

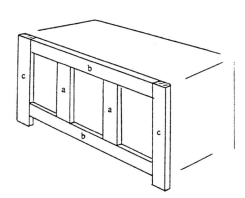

Fig. 43
Working on a frame.
Innermost pieces first and
work outwards: parts a,
then b and finally c.

is then followed by the lower rails *c*, then the front, rear and side rails *d*. After these the front legs *e*, the top or cresting rail *f*, and finally the rear legs *g*. Regardless of the type of furniture concerned, the same principle applies; work from the centre out.

Fig. 44
Sequence of work on a chair.
Innermost pieces first and
work outwards.

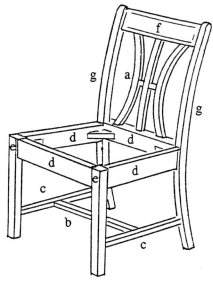

It is important to finish each section accurately on the joint lines, so that when the following section is done, the overlapping is minimal. If overlapping does occur and the polish dries, these places will become double coated. As previously mentioned, this will cause an uneven surface and, although not very noticeable at this stage, will show up more as the finish develops.

If each successive section can be done fairly quickly after the previous one, there is a better chance of each area of polish blending together smoothly. On large pieces of work where this is not possible, accuracy is even more important.

Where the section being dealt with is wide, working up to a joint can be done using the same method as described for a small panel, page 96. This is by quickly running along the inside of the joint line at each end before starting to work lengthways.

The above procedure applies to base coats, colouring, and the finishing process. **It is not necessary to work to joint lines during the course of bodying-up when there is oil present.** At this stage the rubber can be worked freely over the surface.

The comments in the previous section apply to the joint lines on frames, and must not be confused with the joints on wide, flat surfaces. Many surfaces, such as table tops, the sides and tops of cabinets, etc, are made up of pieces of wood running in different directions. This may be due to the type of construction or, in the case of decorative veneered surfaces, to the various pieces of veneer that make up the pattern. In these situations, polishing is normally carried out in one direction, just as if it were a plain board with the grain all going one way. Obviously you have to decide which way you are going to work, and this usually follows the length of the piece concerned as opposed to the width. Fig. 45 is an example of this situation. This is the "fall" (hinged top) of a bureau, and at each end there is a piece of wood running at 90° to the main board.

Polishing should be carried out following the longest sides as indicated by the arrows.

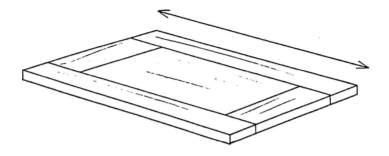

Fig. 45 *It is not necessary to work to joint lines on a wide, flat surface. The direction of work normally follows the longest sides.*

Working to a Stopped End

An example of this would be the rear of a chair frame where the cross rail meets the uprights. Fig. 46. Exactly the same principle applies as when working inside a frame, page 96. Work the tip of the rubber up and down at the end of the rail, going off the edges of course. Do this at both ends quickly and then run along the length before the polish at each end has dried.

When eventually doing the upright part, the narrow surface (*a*) should be done with the very tip of the rubber, so as to avoid getting polish on the cross rail, otherwise double coating will occur and the quality will suffer. Fig. 47 shows the rubber strokes necessary when working around a cross rail in this way. First work the tip of the rubber two short strokes above and below the rail. Then the narrow surface (*a*). Work from the centre out in both cases, so that if you

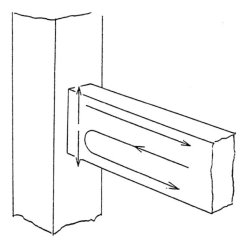

Fig. 46 *Use the tip of the rubber and make sure that it is going off at the edges and not onto them.*

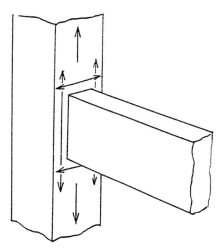

Fig. 47 *Use the tip of the rubber here also. Try not to touch the cross rail. The rubber must not be too wet.*

catch the rail you will be working **off the edge,** which will avoid runs being produced. The main rubbering of each side of the rail can then continue.

Keeping the Edge Wet

The reason that we apply french polish in strips is in order to blend the polish together into a flat, even layer. As each strip meets the previous one, it overlaps a little and blends together smoothly because the previous strip has not had time to dry. This is called "keeping the edge wet", and is very important towards producing a consistent surface. This is why we never apply french polish in squares, as in painting. If we did, by the time we had worked from one square to another, much of the polish would have dried and the joints would then be double coated.

Bodying-Up

For the purpose of prescribing a straightforward system, I have based the amount of bodying-up carried out upon five sets of circles at a time. This is a reasonable number for the beginner to get used to. However, there is nothing wrong with either increasing or decreasing this a little, depending upon the finish required. This choice will become easier as experience is gained. It is important, though, to be aware of the fact that, if too much bodying-up is done without resting the work, the methylated spirit in the polish does not have time to evaporate sufficiently. Owing to this, the surface will remain soft and fairly vulnerable. In this situation there is the possibility of the surface being torn by the rubber, particularly if there is not enough oil present. In its lightest form this sort of damage shows up as dull streaks. A little worse and you could have severe circular rubber marks, and the worst scenario is when parts of the surface are actually pulled up by the rubber. If there is any indication at all that this might be happening, put everything down, walk well away and go and watch Coronation Street for half an hour. The worst thing you can do is to try to rectify it straight away. In fact, this applies to most things where french polishing is concerned. If you feel that something is starting to go a little wrong, leave it alone before too much damage is done and then return later with a fresh mind.

Going back to numbers of circles, ten sets at a time is a reasonable maximum.

Slapping
What a wonderful heading to finish off this section!

This is not a technique but more a habit. After re-charging the rubber and squashing out, but before applying the oil, I tend, by habit, to slap the rubber lightly into the palm of the left hand. I have also seen other professionals doing this. I think that this stems from the desire, even after squashing out well, to make sure that there is no excessive wetness on the face of the rubber.

VENEERED WORK

If you are presented with a piece of veneered work to polish, including marquetry, it is advisable to thoroughly examine the whole surface before polishing begins. This is to check for small areas of loose veneer that may not have adhered properly. The Furniture Maker will obviously have done this, but a double check is well worth the time.

This is carried out by running one's finger tips over the surface and carefully listening for a change in sound. Other indications may be either a slight hump or a slight hollow on the surface. Careful positioning of a lamp shining across the surface will also help to show up faults such as these. Once a suspect place has been found, the actual size of the unglued area can be more accurately assessed by tapping around it with the finger nail. At this point, a definite change in sound will be noticed and the position can then be marked lightly with a pencil. It is also advisable to stick a small piece of masking tape adjacent to each area. By doing this, none will be forgotten. Detecting these loose areas is essential, otherwise, when the work is finished, they show up as blisters.

It is well to check all veneered work in this manner, whether it is new or an existing piece of furniture. There is nothing more infuriating than finding these blisters when you are three quarters of the way through the polishing process.

Rectification is not too difficult but care is necessary. The object is to get glue underneath the surface. To do this, two craft knives are required. Cut the veneer gently across the centre of the blister and in line with the grain. Carefully slip the tip of a knife underneath and lift the veneer a little. Pick up a small amount of glue with the tip of the other knife, gently slide it in and deposit the glue under the surface. If the veneer is lifted up and down a few times, this will help to spread the glue as far as possible. Repeat this once or twice until you are sure that there is plenty of glue present, and then do the same on the other side of the slit. After wiping off the surplus glue with a damp cloth, the area must be pressed flat with a small wooden block, held with either a suitable cramp or a weight. Place a piece of thin plastic sheet down first to prevent the block from sticking to the surface (plastic carrier bag) and then put the block in position. I personally find that Cascamite resin glue works well for this purpose. It should not be mixed too thickly (about the thickness of single cream).

If you are repairing veneer on a polished surface, make sure that the area is completely dry after wiping off the surplus glue, otherwise moisture will be trapped underneath the plastic sheet and this would very likely cause a white mark.

CLEANING THE HANDS

It is inevitable that you will get polish on your hands. The only way to avoid this is to wear disposable gloves. (Page 45) French polish, of course, can be softened with methylated spirit, but I would not recommend this for hand cleaning. A good method is to soak the hands for 3 to 4 minutes in a bowl of hot water, into which a bar of soap has been placed and also a small piece of cloth. After a few minutes you can start to rub the polish off with the cloth. This does take a little time, and patience is necessary. A way of speeding this up is to use a small amount of washing soda (about a teaspoonful) instead of soap. Although this is effective, I could not recommend it for general use owing to the fact that some people have sensitive skin, and contact with washing soda may lead to skin problems. Incidentally, washing soda must not be confused with caustic soda. **Caustic soda is extremely dangerous and should not be used under any circumstances.** Before leaving the subject of hands, barrier creams are very useful. If rubbed well in before polishing is started they make cleaning of the hands afterwards much easier.

COATING WITH A BRUSH

Although I prefer to do most of my work with a rubber, there are, of course, bound to be exceptions. For example, the inside of cupboards that require only a very simple finish.

This can be accomplished by applying a brush coat of polish or sanding sealer. After it has hardened sufficiently, it is eased down with a medium grade paper and then, to finish off, either another coat or a rubber of polish is applied. This could be repeated if the wood is very porous. Only a good quality polisher's mop should be used for coating. A size 12 or 14 is useful for this sort of work unless very large areas are envisaged. (Photograph opposite page 48)

Brush coating should be done in strips in the same way that a rubber is used. The principle is the same, and each strip must join the previous one before it has had time to dry. Obviously, one must be extremely careful not to produce runs. When coating flat open surfaces, as with a rubber; **always go off at an edge, never on to an edge.** The polish mix can be thicker for brushing, approximately ten parts polish to one part methylated spirit would be a good starting point.

Sanding sealer, incidentally, is french polish (usually white) with a very fine chalk powder mixed in with it. It penetrates the grain and helps to fill up the porous surface. Also, when hard, it is very easy to sand, hence its name.

BLEACHING

Occasionally, it is necessary to use wood bleach as a means of removing marks and stains. Oxalic acid has been the traditional bleach to use for this purpose for many years. It is, however, fairly difficult to obtain nowadays and great care is needed when using it, as it is poisonous. In addition to this, it can be absorbed through the skin, so gloves must be worn. Oxalic acid comes in the form of fine white crystals. A teaspoonful dissolved in a third of a jam jar of hot water will give a good useable strength. Mark the jar and the container with the crystals in "POISON" and keep out of the reach of children. Wood bleaches will only work on bare wood and it is important that the surface is clean if a good result is to be achieved.

Apart from oxalic acid there are a few proprietary single-liquid wood bleaches on the market and also some two-pack products. The single-liquid bleaches are usually a type of strong acid and will remove or improve grey or black marks caused by water staining. They will not normally lighten the wood. They may appear to, but what is really happening is a sort of super cleaning process. Two-pack bleaches are usually based upon peroxide and these will, in most cases, lighten the colour of the wood itself. However, there is a disadvantage (Isn't there always?) in that these chemicals are very hazardous to use.

When working on ring marks, apply the bleach carefully with the tip of a small brush to the mark only. If the bleach gets onto the unmarked surface, it will probably clean it and the result then will start to become patchy. Always apply bleaches using a brush, never a cloth. Avoid letting the metal part of the brush come into contact with the bleach, as the chemical reaction produced could reduce its strength. For two-pack bleaches, special brushes are sometimes required.

If a second application is necessary, wait until the first coat is completely dry. Bleaches should always be left to dry thoroughly as they will carry on working for quite a while after they are applied.

One of the problems of using wood bleaches is that after using them you must wash away all traces from the surface. The reason for this, and in particular when oxalic acid is used, is that if left in the grain it will ultimately cause the polish to deteriorate. The surface should first be washed with neat vinegar and dried off. (Ordinary household vinegar is fine.) This is followed by vinegar and water, and then water on its own. Never leave the surface wet for any length of time and carefully dispose of all rags used.

Cleaning, as above, should be carried out after most bleaching operations unless otherwise stated by the manufacturer. Never use metal objects or steel wool when bleaching, as these will react with the chemicals and cause black stains on the wood.

Be careful with veneered work. The presence of water can soften the glue and cause veneers to lift.

Please do not be under the illusion that because proprietary bleaches are packaged, whether single or two-pack, in smart containers they are fairly safe to use. These products are, by their very nature, extremely strong chemicals. Wear gloves and goggles, read the safety warnings and avoid contact with the skin.

Well, I suppose you are now wondering, "Is it really worth it?" In many cases it just isn't. In fact, if the piece of furniture that you are working on is quite old, a few small ring marks here and there will often produce a little bit of character or "history" as we say.

HOLDING THE WORK

One of the main problems associated with french polishing is that of holding the work. I have included in the following pages a few methods and ideas that are often useful. A fair amount of ingenuity is required, as there is obviously a good deal of variety in furniture design.

New furniture poses a particular problem. Should it be polished before assembly or afterwards? Let us take as an example a simple open fronted bookcase as shown in Fig. 48.

Fig. 48
A simple bookcase.
A better job can be made
of the inside surfaces if
polished before assembly.

If polished after assembly the outside surfaces would be easy to work on, but the shelves and other places inside quite difficult. You would be constantly working into corners, and producing both an even staining and an even finish would be hard to achieve. On the other hand, if polished before assembly the staining and polishing would be easier, but there would be a holding problem. In addition to this, a number of the components need to be finished on both sides.

As with many things, the best course is a compromise between the two, and in this situation it would be best to polish the inside surfaces first, and then the outside ones after assembly. An important point to bear in mind here, is that one has to be careful not to get stain, grain-filler or polish onto the surfaces of any joints that are to be glued together. It is best to cover these surfaces with masking tape before work is started.

The following ideas will hopefully provide methods that can either be used or modified to suit a variety of situations.

Flat Surfaces

There are two main difficulties where flat surfaces are concerned. Firstly, they will slide around if not held firmly; and secondly, it is often necessary to polish both sides. In some cases one side can be done and then left to harden for a few days before doing the other one. In this situation the finished side, which will be face down, should be placed on soft bench pads, Fig. 49. These are wooden strips onto which a soft surface has been glued. Strips of carpet are ideal for this purpose. It is best to use an off-cut of new carpet in order to make sure that there is no dust or grit present. Never leave a piece of polished work on the bench pads for any length of time. Even though the surface might have had a few days to harden, prolonged pressure, no matter how light, will inevitably form a mark. As previously mentioned, a polished surface will take several weeks to cure properly. A fairly good way of storing pieces during the course of polishing, is to lean them against the wall on top of a bench or table, Fig. 50.

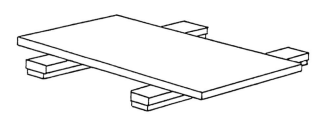

Fig. 49   *Working on bench pads. Make sure the top surfaces*
are clean and free from dust and grit.

Fig. 50
When placing components
aside to harden, keep them
clear of the bench and the
wall with small strips of
wood.

Two strips of wood are placed underneath to raise the
component off the surface, and a smaller one at the top will prevent
it from touching the wall. Even on bench pads, panels will tend to
slide around. A simple method of holding them is shown in Fig. 51
using a few pieces of scrap wood nailed together.

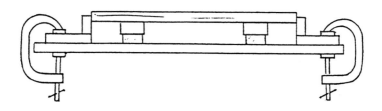

Fig. 51 *Holding a flat piece of work still. This method is easily adjusted for different sizes.*

It is important that the top of the block at each end is below the level of the panel, so that the rubber can run off unrestricted.

Sometimes time is of the essence and you cannot wait for one side to harden before doing the other side. A method that I have often used in this situation is to attach extension pieces to each end of the panel with some long thin screws. Fig. 52.

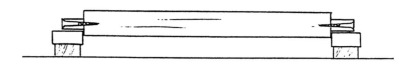

Fig. 52 *Using extension pieces. Care must be taken not to apply excessive downwards pressure. Otherwise this may cause the wood to split.*

The extension pieces need to be thinner than the workpiece, so, as with the previous example, the rubber can leave the end of the work without being obstructed. Obviously, this method is only possible if the edges are not to be polished.

If only one side of a panel or board is to be polished, mounting it on a base board as shown in Fig. 53 is well worth the effort. The spacing block can be fastened to the baseboard using panel pins, and then the workpiece attached with four pieces of double sided tape.

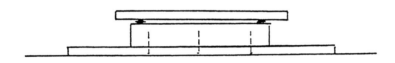

Fig. 53 *The spacing block should be smaller than the workpiece itself so that the edges can be worked upon easily.*

Small components, such as those found dividing up compartments inside a bureau, can often be difficult to hold. Fig. 54 shows a simple method of working on both sides by using a couple of panel pins at each end. These pieces can then be picked up and placed against the wall to harden in a similar way to Fig. 50.

Fig. 54
The use of panel pins
in the ends of small
components makes
them easier to handle.
Drill small pilot holes
to avoid splitting the ends.

Small box-type objects such as jewellery boxes and their lids often prove awkward. The best way I have found of dealing with such items is to fasten them to a large block of wood (once again with four pieces of double-sided tape), the block itself having previously been fixed to a board. Fig. 55. I have found double sided tape very useful for these purposes. Blu-Tack could also be used, or alternatively small spots of glue from a hot melt glue gun.

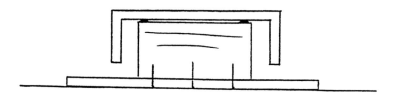

Fig. 55 *The double sided tape usually needs to be folded*
over several times and made into small pads in order
to allow for any slight unevenness of the surface.

When working on turned work and, in particular, small items, it is necessary to be able to work all the way round and at the same time hold the turning quite firmly. With the aid of a few bits of old copper tube begged off your local plumber, this can be done as shown in Fig. 56.

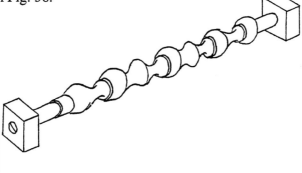

Fig. 56 *A method of holding turned work using copper tubing and long screws.*

The copper tube is used as a handle and fastened with a long thin screw through a small wooden block. A simple rack can be made for holding such work. Support pieces are attached to a base board and notches are cut out as shown in Fig. 57. A further

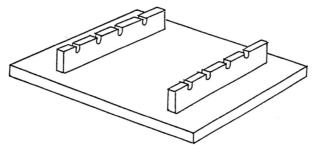

Fig. 57 *The front notches can be used for polishing and the rear ones for leaving the work to harden.*

refinement here is to cut a few pointed teeth on the inner end of the tubes; this will provide a more positive grip.

Small parts that are held with dowels, such as the finials on Viennese wall clocks, can be placed on a peg board made out of a piece of scrap wood, Fig. 58.

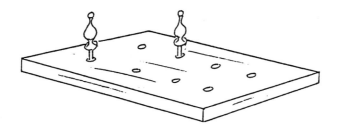

Fig 58 *A fairly loose fit is best so that each item can be picked up easily.*

The methods shown here are only a few examples of different ways of holding components, but hopefully they will charge the imagination.

SURFACE DAMAGE

Ring Marks; Blemishes;
Effects of Heat; Scratches;
Cigarette Burns

When re-polishing a piece of furniture it is often necessary to deal with certain surface defects first. Those included here tend to be the most common ones that need attention.

White Ring Marks

These are caused by either moisture or the combination of heat and moisture. When a hot mug or plate is put down onto a polished surface, the heat forces moisture in the form of vapour into the finish which causes a "bloom" or whiteness on the surface. A slower permeation of moisture in the form of water will also have a similar effect. An example of this is when watering a vase of flowers. If a small amount of water trickles down the outside unnoticed, it will eventually find its way underneath and, if left for several days, will form a white mark.

In many cases the actual depth of the damage is quite small, only a few thousandths of an inch, and rectification can often be achieved by carefully removing a little of the surface with a fine polishing abrasive such as rottenstone powder. There are, however, some dangers to consider before attempting this. First of all, it is impossible to tell how deep the mark is before starting work, and secondly, a remedy of this type should only be carried out on a surface that has a shine and not a modern matt or satin finish. The reason for this is that rubbing the surface with a fine abrasive will produce a high shine, and this could look a little odd in the middle of a modern matt finished dining table. (Clearly a job for an expert!)

White marks that have had long term exposure do tend to be deeper and are often accompanied by a black mark that has developed underneath. A simple remedy in this sort of case may not be possible, and stripping might be necessary. If the piece of furniture concerned has any value, whether in terms of money or sentimental value, please consult an expert first. (Repeating myself again!)

Let us suppose, though, that the mark is shallow and polishing it out is to be considered. It is important that this is only attempted on a surface that is intact and not cracked, otherwise the polishing compound will find its way into the cracks and leave a mark. The best way to use rottenstone for this purpose is to sprinkle a small amount onto the surface, and gently rub with a cloth moistened with a little white spirit. It is usually necessary to repeat this several times. I have heard of other fine abrasives being used for this purpose; for example, liquid metal polish and even cigarette ash for very minor problems. Metal polish works well, but do make sure, as mentioned above, that the surface is completely intact and with a fairly full finish, as metal polish should not be allowed under any circumstances to penetrate the surface of the wood itself. An additional disadvantage with metal polish is that if the finish is not completely full it will dry out and show up white in the grain, which may end up looking worse than the original problem. This can, however, sometimes be corrected by washing the surface with white spirit, and after this is dry using a coloured wax polish. It usually works, but not always!

General Blemishes

These might include such things as light water damage that has dulled the surface but has not gone white, and also the result of spilt spirits that may have eroded the surface a little and left a mark. In general, and providing it is not too severe, this sort of light damage will disappear with cleaning and re-polishing. A good way of testing for this is to lightly wipe the surface with white spirit. If the marks become invisible, re-polishing will usually have the same effect. Often the surface over such blemishes is a little coarse to the touch, and it may be necessary to very lightly smooth the area using fine steel wool and white spirit. This must be done very gently, particularly if wax polishing is to follow as opposed to french polishing, otherwise the surface may become scratched.

Effects of Heat

In this context I am referring to the damage caused by a piece of furniture being too close to a heat source such as a fire. Chair and table legs seem to be the two worst sufferers in this respect. Such areas are identified by a general coarseness and usually dozens of very tiny, almost microscopic blisters. This can also manifest itself as surface crazing and, in severe cases, the finish may even be charred. The way we deal with this depends upon the degree of damage. If it is of a reasonably light nature, a gentle rub with white spirit and fine steel wool (0000 grade) will remove the coarseness and the surface can then be re-polished. Where the damage is severe, it may be necessary to strip the section concerned, but before embarking upon this there is another solution that can be tried first. This is to gently rub the affected area with a cloth moistened with methylated spirit. If the existing finish is french polish, doing this will help to soften and re-amalgamate the surface. Care must be taken to avoid rubbing through to the bare wood. It is best not to dwell too much in one place but work systematically over the whole of the area fairly quickly. The process can be repeated once or twice according to the results achieved. A certain amount of the existing finish will inevitably be removed, but this may still be a better alternative than completely stripping.

Scratches

Very fine surface scratches will usually become invisible during the process of re-polishing, but occasionally, if the existing surface is a modern lacquer, they may not disappear completely. In such a case the best thing to do is to carefully touch them out with spirit colours, after applying the first few rubbers of french polish. (pages 59-63). Deeper scratches pose more of a problem. The normal solution is to fill them with wax filler (page 19) and then adjust the colour with spirit colours once again after a few rubbers of polish have been applied.

Very deep scratches and grooves may have to be dealt with in several stages. The bulk of the damage is filled with woodfiller and then wax filler is used to finish the repair. The woodfiller should be pressed in firmly and then scraped off about one millimetre below the surface. After this has hardened, preferably overnight, the remainder can be filled with wax filler of an appropriate colour. This method is for use on top of existing finishes, in order to avoid the use of coarse sandpaper which would obviously scratch the surface.

Cigarette Burns

Not very nice to deal with and almost impossible to make completely invisible. The burn will usually have caused a depression in the surface and the area will be very dark due to charring.

There are two ways of dealing with a cigarette burn, the choice of which depends largely upon the depth and severity of the damage that has been caused. Small shallow burns can be dealt with by first attending to the colour, and then filling with a transparent filler, this being either wax or shellac based. Deep burns are best filled first and the colour attended to afterwards using normal touching-up techniques.

Let us take a look at a shallow burn to begin with. Before starting work on the colour, it is important to make sure that the surface within the burn is sound. The charred area should be gently scraped with a craft knife and all loose fragments removed. The best way of lightening the colour is by carefully touching it out with a french polish based paint. This is known as "dope" and is made up by mixing powdered earth pigments into a small amount of french polish (Pages 67-68). Once the colour has been adjusted to the surrounding area, the work should be left for a few hours to harden, and then one or two light coats of french polish applied to the repair for extra protection. It should then be left overnight to harden further. After this, the slight hollow caused by the burn can be filled to the surface with natural wax filler. This is a fairly simple repair, but the problem with a large area of wax such as this, is poor adhesion of the subsequent french polish. A better method is to drip transparent shellac filler into the hollow (Page 15). This should be done in stages and, as each application cools, carefully scrape away the surplus with a sharp blade. Finishing off is done carefully with fine sandpaper and a small block. This method, although effective, is tricky to carry out and there is obviously a danger of damaging the surface of the existing finish.

The procedure for repairing a deep burn differs in that the filling is carried out first. Loose fragments are scraped away and the depression filled with woodfiller or shellac stick. It is best to use a filler slightly lighter than the surrounding area and colour it down afterwards, as greater control can be achieved in this way. The surplus filler should once again be carefully scraped away with a knife in order to avoid the use of coarse sandpaper. Final levelling should be done very gently, as before, with fine sandpaper and a small block. After applying one or two thin coats of french polish to seal the surface, colouring can be carried out in the normal way as described in Chapter 5, (pages 59-64).

CLEANING and WAX POLISHING

It is surprising just how effective cleaning and wax polishing can be when a piece of furniture is looking a bit dull and shabby. The method of cleaning in this situation is virtually the same as that described in Chapter 7, but a piece of either coarse cloth or hessian is used instead of steel wool. This is to avoid scratching the surface.

The surface is moistened with a cloth containing white spirit (wearing gloves, of course, Page 72), and then rubbed with the hessian. The hessian can also be moistened a little. For most purposes a piece about eight inches square folded into a small pad is a useful size. Do make sure that the hessian is absolutely clean and does not contain any foreign bodies such as bits of grit, sawdust or indeed anything that may scratch the surface.

After the cleaning has been done the surface should be wiped over using a piece of clean soft cloth. The work must then be left to dry thoroughly (preferably overnight) before wax polishing is started. Sometimes a whitish milky deposit may appear on the surface. This is nothing to be concerned about. It can usually be wiped off, but otherwise will disappear when wax polishing.

In order to build up a little protection, wax polishing should be carried out several times. I always recommend at least five times after a piece of furniture has been cleaned in this way. This may seem a lot, but it is not a lengthy process. The procedure is the same as that described on Page 70. Leave for at least two hours between applications, longer if possible. In fact, one application a day for a few days is ideal. Make sure there is plenty of ventilation when cleaning, and put several layers of newspaper under feet and legs when both cleaning and polishing. After the cleaning has been done, remove the soiled newspapers straight away and replace them with fresh ones, otherwise white spirit may soak through onto the floor.

As far as routine maintenance is concerned, unless a piece of furniture is subjected to very heavy wear and tear, a good wax polishing every six to twelve months is usually quite adequate; and if time permits, in between, the occasional light polish with a furniture cream.

Cleaning and wax polishing, as described above, is only normally necessary every five to ten years. These figures are only approximate, of course, as the need for cleaning obviously varies with each individual situation and depends upon how quickly dust, grime, fingerprints etc. build up on the surface.

When going through the process of a thorough cleaning and re-polishing such as described above, it is always wise to remove metal fittings such as handles, as this will make the work easier and a better result will be achieved. Make sure that the positions of all components and screws are clearly marked so that they can be put back in the same place. The best way I have found of doing this is by using small pieces of masking tape marked with a ballpoint pen.

10

SYSTEMS OF WORK

The following chapter is a summary of the procedures outlined in this book and describes the sequence of producing a range of different finishes. They are numbered from one to six. The first one is a very basic, non-complicated method consisting of using french polish as a sealer and then wax polishing. Although a simple finish, this must not be shunned as inferior, as the result can be very effective in the right circumstances. Finish 2 goes a stage further and includes the filling of holes and colouring. Number 3 is similar but with a fuller appearance. This could be considered as a good standard finish. Number 4 is a full finish which is reduced to s mellow sheen. Number 5 is also a full finish but instead of cutting back the shine, it is retained and then wax polished for extra protection. If a higher shine is required the surface can be burnished before wax polishing. Finally, Number 6 is also fully polished, but in this case the shine is lowered in order to produce either a satin or a matt finish, the degree of which can be adjusted according to the level required.

Terminology varies a little throughout the restoration and wood finishing trades. I will just clarify a few of the expressions that have been included in the text.

A **clear rubber** is one that is charged with polish only, and therefore is not contaminated with oil. Clear rubbers and also those that have oil on them should be kept in separate airtight jars, labelled "clear" and "oil".

Easing down refers to gentle sandpapering with the application of only light pressure using a fine paper, and is intended only to remove the very slight coarseness that sometimes occurs between coats or rubbers of polish. May also be referred to as "de-nibbing".

Cleaning up, on the other hand, refers to sandpapering where a medium grade paper is used and a reasonable pressure applied in order to produce a flat, smooth, clean surface.

Worn sandpaper. Always keep a few pieces of used sandpaper, particularly the finer grades. It is very useful for light easing down and levelling wax filler without abrading the surface too much.

Base coats. I have used the term base coats to keep the terminology fairly simple. One base coat in this context is merely one pass over the surface with a rubber charged with french polish and would normally be referred to as a "rubber of polish".

Pulling. After bodying-up and during the course of removing the oil, there will be some resistance felt due to the lack of lubrication. This is referred to as "pulling" and is a sign that the oil is being taken off the surface.

Tearing-up . This appears as a fuzzing on the surface and can occur when re-polishing an existing piece of furniture. Caused by poor adhesion due to insufficient cleaning.

SYSTEMS OF WORK

Finish Number	Stages
No.1 Very simple finish. Open grain. Low sheen. No grain filling, colour matching or wax filling.	Stages 1 & 4. Leave out wax filling.
No.2 Medium semi-open finish. Some open grain. Mellow sheen. *	All stages except Grain Filling.
No.3 Medium-full finish. Little open grain. Mellow sheen. *	All stages.

Finish Number	Stages
No.4 Full Finish No open grain. Mellow sheen. *	All stages and repeat stage 3 three times or more.
No.5 Full Finish No open grain. Full shine.	All stages and repeat stage 3 three times or more. Leave out cutting back and go on to ordinary wax polishing and burnishing if required.
No.6 Finish with reduced shine.	Stages 1-2-3 & 5.

* The term "mellow sheen" refers to a finish that has been cut back with wax polish and fine steel wool so that it has a slightly more mellow appearance than a full shine.

The systems of work outlined above are made up of five main stages which are presented as separate tables on the following pages 135 to 139. Although they may look a little involved, do bear in mind that most of the operations are in fact carried out very quickly. These systems are based on average results. The amount of work necessary to produce a full finish depends on the type of wood and how porous it is to start with.

STAGE 1
INITIAL PREPARATION

Preliminary Work

Primary Stages

New Wood	Stripped Surfaces	Clean & Re-Polish	Staining	First Three Rubbers	Grain-filling	Fourth Rubber
Fill holes. Clean up with sandpaper - 180 then 320.	Clean after stripping with white spirit & 0000 steel wool. Leave to dry. Ease down with 320 paper & dust.	Clean with white spirit & 0000 steel wool. Leave to dry & go to Stage 2 - wax filling. Also deal with faults, eg. ring marks, scratches, heat marks etc.	First - Carry out stain test. Water & Oil Stains Leave to dry - water overnight; oil 24 hours minimum. Spirit Stain 1/2 hour (use on small areas only)	Three clear rubbers, 15 minute intervals. Ease down & dust between 2nd & 3rd rubbers, 320 grade paper. Polish mix - 4 parts polish / 1 part meths	(if required) Leave overnight to dry. Following day ease down lightly with 400 grade paper, dust & wipe once with methylated spirit.	One clear rubber. Leave for 2 hours before wax filling. If grainfilling has been done this can be reduced to 1 hour. See page 59.

STAGE 2
BASE WORK

Wax Filling	Fifth & Sixth Rubbers	Colour Matching & Touching-Up	Seventh & Eighth Rubbers
(if necessary) Select the correct colour, fill small holes. Level with worn 400 paper & dust.	Two clear rubbers of polish at 15 minute intervals. Leave for 15 minutes before touching-up or colour matching.	(if necessary) Touch-up light spots or patches and colour match larger areas using spirit based colours. Leave to dry for 15 minutes.	Two clear rubbers prior to bodying-up at 15 minute intervals.

STAGE 3
BODYING-UP & FINISHING

←———— Oil Rubber ————→ ←———— Clear Rubber ————→

Applying Oil	Figures of Eight	Circles	Figures of Eight	Removing the Oil		Oil Still Present
4 straight rubbers with oil added. Start from alternate sides. If jet stream does not appear, increase oil a little.	2 sets figures of eight with oil.	5 sets of circles with oil.	2 sets figures of eight. Stop adding oil at this point.	3 straight. Same rubber. No oil. Increase interval gradually to 15 minutes. Set aside to rest if bodying-up again the same day.	Change rubber. 2 straight clear rubbers, 15 minute intervals. Thinner polish 2 : 1 polish : meths. Jet stream gone & pulling. Set aside to rest or harden if finished.	(a jet stream still follows rubber) Make completely fresh rubber & make 2 further passes with an interval of 15 minutes. Set aside to rest or harden if finished.

137

STAGE 4
WAX POLISHING

Cutting back	Extra Protection	Maintenance
Dark wax polish - medium & dark surfaces. Light wax polish - light surfaces. Fine steel wool, grade 0000, once or twice.	4-6 applications light wax polish.	Wax polish once or twice a year all over.

STAGE 5
REDUCTION OF SHINE

Level 1 Mellow Finish	Lightly brush with fine pumice powder.
Level 2 Satin Finish	Rub with oil and fine pumice followed by Rottenstone. Clean the surface with white spirit and then vinegar. Lightly wax polish if necessary.
Level 3 Matt Finish	Rub with oil and fine pumice. Clean surface with white spirit and then vinegar.

Reduction of shine is best carried out on fairly full finishes (ie. Finish nos. 3 & 4). If carried out on open-grain type finishes there is a risk of the pumice powder showing up white in the grain. If this does happen, coloured wax polish will often effect a cure. Alternatively, an application of oil stain applied with a piece of wadding and then rubbed dry is another possible remedy.

APPENDIX 1

A PRACTICE PIECE

A practice piece is the best way of gaining experience before venturing on to a piece of furniture, and for this purpose a piece of blockboard or plywood measuring approximately 24" x 12" (60cm x 30cm) is ideal. The thickness should be at least $1/2$" (12mm) so that the board is fairly rigid. $3/4$" (18mm) blockboard is excellent. If it is a piece of old board that is to be used, it must, of course, first be stripped as detailed in Chapter 8.

A means of holding the board so that it can be worked upon comfortably must be devised. Figs. 59 and 60 show two ways of doing this. If you are lucky enough to have a work bench and a vice, a strip of wood can be fastened to the underside of the board so that it can be held in the vice, Fig, 59. Otherwise, if working on a table, the practice piece can be held as shown in Fig. 60 by screwing two extra pieces of a similar material underneath. These can be clamped to the table with one or two G-cramps. If the table being used is a good one, do please protect the surface with an old blanket or something similar, otherwise you may find you have a large project sooner than expected!

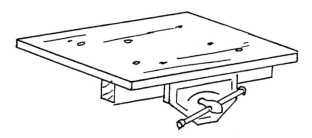

Fig. 59 *Practice board for use in a vice.*

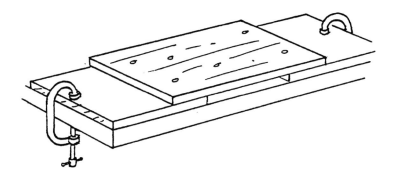

Fig. 60 *Practice board for use on a table top.*

The screws can be put in from above, countersunk, and filled. This will provide good filling and touching-up practice. A number of holes of different sizes are required, and a good way of making these is with the nose of a pair of pliers. Press hard to make about six holes $^3/_{16}$" to $^1/_4$" across (4mm to 6mm) and then gently to make another six smaller ones. These can be scattered about at random. The addition of one or two light scores and scratches will also be of benefit as the object is to simulate a variety of different problems. Another technique that can be practised is the raising of a bruise and this can be produced with the round end of a ball peen hammer.

The larger holes should be filled with woodfiller. The small holes and scratches, however, are left for wax filling at a later stage.

INDEX